THE
RELUCTANT
CHANNEL

THE
RELUCTANT
CHANNEL

A GIFT OF DIVINE WISDOM

BY

Helenne Deutscher
& C P Beauvoir

ISBN-10: 0-9975066-1-X
ISBN-13: 978-0-9975066-1-7

Book Cover Design & Formatting by Damonza
Book Editing by Brenda Errichiello from Forest North Books

www.HelenneDeutscher.com
www.cpbeauvoir.com

CONTENTS

PREFACE

I'M A SEVENTY-TWO-YEAR-OLD woman who has lived most of my life in fear. I was afraid of who I was, afraid of who I wasn't. I was afraid of life, afraid of death, afraid of existing, afraid of surviving, afraid of being. I was afraid of knowing my purpose and even more afraid of being oblivious to it. I was scared of anything and everything. Fear and anxiety were my constant companions.

The only thing that scared me more than being afraid was the thought of not being afraid. My fears left me feeling paralyzed, believing that I was a freak and that most people would never understand me. Nor would they ever truly like me. In my desperation to feel loved, I used food, shopping, and drugs to fill the void within my heart. But the hole within me could never be filled. I went out into the world, searching for anything that could complete me. I searched and searched, but nothing I found ever lasted. I would hence be temporarily relieved, a sense of peace lurking over me, but sooner or later, this peaceful feeling would disappear and I was left to return to my dysfunctional patterns, alone and vulnerable.

I did not know how to love myself. The only thing I knew, the only thing I excelled at, was doing a great job at hating me—and I did it well! I hated my body, hated the way I looked. I hated the things I said, hated the things I did not say. I hated the things I did and hated even more the things I did not do. Nothing I did was good enough. Nothing I was was good enough. From mind, body, and soul, I was the exact definition of a wreck. I was my own worst enemy, spending most of my time being the faithful passenger of a destructive emotional rollercoaster where extreme highs and lows were the norms. During this vicious rollercoaster ride that was my life, I experienced bouts of severe anxiety and depression and I constantly thought of suicide. I once came very close to ending my life.

The night I almost killed myself, I was very weary. Everything was hurting badly. I felt the pain throughout all the cells in my body. It was in my muscles, my bones, my mind, my heart. Even my soul was hurting. I remember staring at the bottle of pills that I was holding in my hand and though I did not go through with it, I took comfort in the thought that if things got more difficult, I didn't have to stay here and suffer. I had a way out. And so, when it was revealed to me that I would be writing this book, I immediately asked myself: Who was

I to be writing a book, and who in the world would want to read it?

It was at the age of forty-seven that I met Tomas, my angelic, spiritual guide. I saw him clearly, heard him speak to me, felt his energy. The spiritual concepts in this book have been taught to me by him. I remember the day Tomas told me I was a gift. I cringed, thinking he was crazy. An uncomfortable chill ran down my spine, sending a wave of anxiety down my back. I then laughed and became very angry. I didn't like nor could I grasp the concept of being a gift. As far as I was concerned, I was a mess, and anyone who hung out with me was a mess too. How could I, who hated everything about myself, even consider the thought of being a gift? Did Tomas not know who I was?

I, Helenne Deutscher, was far from being a gift. I had such low self-esteem that I consistently tried to destroy the person I thought I was. And every time I went on the path of self-destruction, guilt and shame consumed me like a thick fog, blinding my sight. I could not see clearly unless I punished myself for being so bad. But no punishment was ever enough. I was my most devoted accuser, judge, and executioner. I wasn't a gift. I couldn't be. And I couldn't allow myself to think, or to believe that there would be a day when I would actually see myself as such—until, moment by moment, day by day, Tomas begun teaching me how to live life the way God intended for it to be. A life of peace, joy, prosperity, and love.

Who am I to be writing this book?

I, Helenne Deutscher, am a child of God, created in truth. With the help of my spiritual guide, I discovered the true God in me and who I truly am. My life has changed tremendously since the day I met Tomas, and this book is about the lessons I've learned throughout my journey as a trance channel as I struggled to accept the very things I did not believe I deserved.

I, Helenne Deutscher, am a daughter of the Universe, created in God's power, energy, and love. My service here is to deliver the messages that have been taught to me in their original and pure state. I am a vehicle in service to God as a messenger of love to help my brothers and sisters rediscover their connection to the Source of All: God.

I, Helenne Deutscher, am a gift, a creation of the Supreme Creator. I have discovered how to live a fulfilling life and it is my great pleasure to share with you how you can do the same if you so choose. May the teachings in this book help you remove the blocks that are standing in your way in order to allow the blessings that are here for you to manifest in your life. Tomas has helped me achieve my heart's desire, and I pray that this book will do the same for you.

A MESSAGE FROM TOMAS

DEEP WITHIN EACH being is a door—a golden door. We have no conscious memory of it. Yet know that as you are reading this now, there is a part of you that knows this is the truth. In our travels within our being, we have stood in front of this door without knowing how to get the door to open. There is a keyhole in this door. We know that there is a key, but we do not know how to find it. And no matter what we have done in the past to open this door, nothing we have done has worked. The desire to open and go through this door is deeply rooted within us. We know there is a great treasure that lies behind this golden door—if only we could find the key to gain entrance.

My dear ones, I will now tell you where the key is that you are desperately searching for. The key to this door resides within you. The only way that you will find it is to go within yourself. Start the journey of finding you, by seeing all of your flaws revealed to you. Learn to love yourself unconditionally, no matter what you do or do not do, as God always loves you. That, my child, is the key that opens the door. Nothing else. No substitute will work.

Once this door opens, a whole new world and life will unfold in front of you. You will experience the gifts of peace and joy without overreacting to the situations of life. You will know yourself and so you will know God. What you give to yourself is directly given to the Father in Heaven, the Source of All, God, as well. May you feel the love that resides in the pages of this book and experience the wonders of peace and joy. You have no idea how much we, who are in Spirit, love you. We are here to serve you.

In love,

Tomas

PART ONE

THE PUZZLE
OF HELENNE

"My name is Tomas, spelled T-O-M-A-S. Not Thomas. Tomas is my name."

CHAPTER 1

MEETING TOMAS

I T HAPPENED ON October 6, 1990, the day after my forty-seventh birthday. I woke up on that morning feeling down. It's like the day after your birthday, the party's over and reality sets in. On that morning, I was thinking: "I'm an older woman—and look at me. I hate my job. I'm stressed about my finances, yet I continue to buy more things and remain in debt. I wish I could go away and start a new life. Someplace that's nice and quiet, where the trees are tall, the leaves green, the flowers fully open, embracing the morning's sunlight. I wish to go someplace where I won't feel like I'm a failure, where I can forget about this reality, where I can just live a fun, happy life. But I can't go anywhere—I'm stuck. I'm stuck with this life, stuck with my debts, stuck with my depressed thoughts. It's not just a reality. It's my reality. And there's no place where I can escape where my reality won't follow."

I forced myself to get out of bed and I walked to the living room, where I could easily look out of the window. From where I stood, I could see the beautiful blue sky and white puffy clouds. And just like that, my attention was redirected to the positive. It was another bright and sunny day. And as I gazed out the window, I felt a strong pull to get out and go relax on the beach. The beach has always been a healing place for me. It has always been one of my favorite places to go to regenerate. When I go to the beach, I feel calm, serene, and completely at peace. It's like taking a deep breath of fresh air, letting it cleanse the insides of my body, releasing it and becoming a whole new person in the process. It truly is an amazing feeling. Without another thought, I gathered myself together, threw on my bathing suit and wrap, grabbed my beach umbrella, towels, and beach chair and out the door I scampered.

Being that it was an early morning, not many people were on the beach that day. It was just the perfect day to sit, relax, and let time pass by. As I crossed the boardwalk and reached the beach, I put my bare feet in the cozy, warm sand where I stood, looking out at the clear blue water with an endless view reaching the lighter blue sky. It was all so beautiful. I paused to admire the view. I wanted to take it all in. I watched the waves roll softly onto the sand and took another long, deep cleansing breath. My lips curved into a bright smile as the air deflated from my lungs. I was so glad to be here! In that moment, I realized that I didn't need to go somewhere far away. The beach was my little getaway. It was my little piece of heaven on Earth.

I walked closer to the familiar place where I usually set up my beach umbrella and chair and settled in. As I sat down, a peaceful feeling drifted over me and I heard myself whisper, "This is the life." Earlier that morning, I could not have dreamed that I would be having such a wonderful time. None of it had been planned out, which was what made it so perfect. For a moment, I closed my eyes. A gentle ocean breeze whispered through my hair as the warmth of the sun caressed my body. I was not meditating. I was simply relaxing, absorbing the warmth and listening to the ocean whisper with each wave gliding over the sand. It was so peaceful.

Suddenly, I was somewhere else!

My eyes beheld a vision of me walking barefoot on a clean white path, wearing a soft white cotton shift. I was drawn to a bright, white, luminous wall with an amazing crystal door in it. I stood in front of this massive crystal door, fascinated by the sparkling light that emanated from within and radiated around it. I had a feeling that all I had to do was be willing to enter, and just with the thought of that willingness, the door opened wide with a smooth glide. I stepped slowly through the door and saw a beautiful garden filled with many magnificent, colorful flowers of all kinds. The colors were rich and impressive, the smell heavenly fragrant. Some I recognized, others I did not.

I continued to walk through the beautiful garden, looking all around. There was a grassy path leading to a grove of trees—rich green trees of all kinds. The way they were growing reminded me of unique bouquets. They were absolutely gorgeous. Beyond the trees, there was a spectacular golden horizon, where a great mountain sat. The mountain looked like it was made of white crystals. There was a soft rosy light shining from the top of the mountain. It was coming from another crystal that was shaped like a castle. I followed the winding path up the mountain and came to the crystal wall of the castle. In the middle of the wall, there was a door—a huge golden door. In my mind, I again felt very willing to enter, and with that thought the door swung open, slowly and silently.

My eyes scanned the room. It was breathtakingly beautiful, made of nothing but crystals. Soft, creamy crystal walls stretched up to a very high ceiling with flowing colors. The floor, also made of crystal, felt comfortably cool to my feet. The room was full of colors so rich and luminous, I felt as though I had never seen them before. To my left there were shelves reaching from floor to ceiling. They were made with the same crystal, filled with books of all sizes and colors. To my right was an exquisite long crystal table. I saw three beings sitting there, dressed in white robes with hoods on their heads, covering their faces.

I took a long look at them, but a brightness of light prevented me from seeing their faces. I kept looking, but their faces remained hidden to me. Then, I heard a rich, deep voice speaking to me telepathically. "We are THE THREE," the voice said through my mind, "and we will be your guides." I immediately thought, "What does that mean?" Without a second passing by, the voice explained that before THE THREE worked directly with me, I would be given a preparation guide and that they would follow after the first one. As the voice was speaking through my mind, a very large American Indian man appeared in front of me. He had a bright, multi-colored blanket over his right shoulder. When he addressed me, he said, "My name is Tomas, spelled T-O-M-A-S. Not Thomas. Tomas is my name." He repeated this to me over and over again, spelling out his name six or seven times. I stared at him, frozen in place.

With an abrupt thud, I was removed.

I immediately opened my eyes, looking around frantically. I quickly realized that I was no longer in the crystal room. I was at the beach. A surge of emotions rushed through me. I felt confused, frightened, and greatly disturbed. I had never experienced anything like that in my life. I was completely and totally freaked out. The only thing I could think of was to get the hell out of there. Quickly jumping up, I began to gather up all my things.

Questions rushed through my mind as fast as a rocket launching into space. What was that, what was that, what in the world was that? What am I to do with it? What was that? What was that? WHAT IN THE WORLD WAS THAT?

For some unknown reason the chatter in my mind brusquely stopped. I glanced down to the beige sand, where something caught my attention. It took a moment for my eyes to focus on the object laying on the sand but there it was: a perfectly curled, variegated, beige-colored shell at my feet. Surprisingly, it was not the kind of shell you would normally find on this beach. I felt it was a sign of good fortune. Quickly, I picked up the shell, grabbed my other stuff, and ran to my car.

On the way home, I kept asking myself, what was that all about? What just happened to me? When I arrived home, I couldn't get the door of my condo to open, and when I looked down I noticed that my hands were shaking violently. I could feel my heart pounding against my chest, the air puffing in and out of my lungs. I felt disoriented, like the ground was shaking beneath my feet and that everything around me was moving uncontrollably. I tried to breathe more calmly, attempting to stop the shaking that was happening in and around me. I'm not sure how I made it in, but once inside I laid everything on the floor and tried to calm my nerves. But I could not.

What in the world was that? What did it all mean? What will happen next? These were the only questions in my mind, and I didn't have a clue on where to find the answers. I was afraid, full of fear, completely terrorized. For the first time in my life, at forty-seven years old, I had experienced something that left me more afraid than fear itself. For the first time in my life, I had experienced something that left me more afraid than my greatest fear: being without fear.

"Fear itself isn't real. It is our belief in it that makes it real."

CHAPTER 2

A WALK THROUGH FEAR

I WAS BORN during World War II, seventeen years after my brother, Irwin. My parents were older, and I was raised as an only child. I didn't really know my brother. I never had an opportunity to form a relationship with him. As far as I knew, Irwin was another adult in the family who lived away from the family home. My parents seldom talked about him, but I was always curious about type of person he was. As I grew a little older, I questioned my mother about Irwin. Besides knowing he was married and living his own life, my brother was a mystery to me. Mother told me Irwin ran away from home at the age of sixteen to join the Marine Corps and that he had come to the hospital to drive us home when I was born. I can still see the smile on my mother's face when she said that the staff at the hospital thought Irwin was her husband

11

and not her son. I can still hear the pride bursting through her voice.

Throughout most of my childhood, I felt and believed I was adopted by my parents. In my child-like mind, I believed I was the secret love child of my brother. I questioned my mother about this on several occasions and each time she assured me that I was her and my father's biological child. Not Irwin's. It took many years of questioning until I was convinced that my mother was telling the truth. Growing up, I wasn't sure where this belief had originated. But in my adult years, I have come to understand why my childhood-self had wanted to be my brother's child. I am the survivor of a dysfunctional home whose foundation was built on abuse, its walls built with severe traumatic experiences. Little Helenne had wanted her brother to be her knight in shining armor. She had wanted her brother to rescue her from the hell that was her home and whisk her away to happily ever after.

Irwin was the saint my mother worshiped. I, on the other hand, was the sinner she tolerated on the good days. On the bad days, I was the catalyst of her rage; I was the failure she chased with wire coat hangers, mop handles, whatever objects were near. I would flee to the nearest room, holding the door with all the strength I had. I feared greatly for my life. When Mother acted like this, there was no doubt in my mind she wanted to kill me. I could see the fire burning in her eyes. I could feel the anger coursing through her. The fury beaming through her was so strong that I could feel my own body heating up. The temperature in the room would get hotter and hotter each time she screamed. Mother was coming for me. She was coming and she was gonna get me. With such knowledge came great responsibility. I used all the strength in my body to keep the door closed, pressing against it with the small of my back. Under no circumstances would I let Mother catch me. I needed to be quick, quicker than her. I needed to be strong, stronger than she was.

From childhood to my teenage years and even into adulthood, I spent a great deal of time wondering why my mother hated me so much, why the sight of me repulsed her, why I could never do anything right in her eyes. I never questioned her about any of this. I just let her be. Mother never failed to remind me of all the ways I came up short. Comparing me to Irwin was one of her favorite pastimes. According to her, Irwin was smarter, funnier, and better than me in all the ways that counted. I barely knew my brother and did not have proof that any of this was true. But as a child, I believed every word Mother had said. She was my mother and I believed she knew best.

My father was a conservative man and quite mellow. He did what he could to protect me from my mother, and I loved him for it. Father was my shelter, always calming the violent storms between Mother and me. My father loved spoiling me with everything I wanted. He was my childhood hero. Or so I thought!

I was well into my fifties when I started to remember certain things about my father that were very disturbing to me. These memories were like an unforeseen earthquake, passing through me, shaking the core of my being. They left me feeling hurt and broken, without a clue about how to puzzle back together the shattered pieces of my life. Growing up, I had the profound belief that it was my mother and not my father who had been the awful one. But then the painful memories about my father surfaced and I got to see that the man I called hero had abused me sexually, mentally, and emotionally. Finding out that my childhood hero wasn't a hero was not the part that hurt most. The part that hurt most was realizing that my hero was in fact a villain in disguise. There is no escaping the pain when that happens. The realization is a sharp knife that cuts right through the heart. And the heart, as strong as it is, is left with no choice but to bleed.

I was four years old when I had my first near-death experience. I became ill and was rushed to the hospital for emergency surgery to remove my appendix. I remember the many faces at the hospital that were glaring at me. Though everyone had facial features that were unique to their ethnicities, the expression on their faces was the same. Being so young, I didn't know what fear looked like. I didn't know how to describe it. I didn't even know what fear was or how it came into existence. But I do remember being put to sleep and overhearing someone say my appendix could burst and I may die. Not long after, I started to drift away, freighted that I was already dying.

I have read many spiritual books. They all talk about freedom. Some of them even talk about freedom from fear. In many of these books, it is written that fear is not real. How could this be? If fear is what I am feeling, how then is it not real? Prior to meeting Tomas, this statement had never felt true to me. The world is a fearful place. The body knows fear. As a matter of fact, if the body is real, then so is fear. I couldn't understand why people were saying that fear wasn't real. When we are afraid, we feel our fears. We may not be able to see the fear, we may not be able to touch the fear, but like the air we breathe, we know it's there. Or is it?

According to Tomas, fear itself isn't real. It is our belief in it that makes it real. Tomas explains that fear is a figment of the ego and it is a lie. It conjures up the untruth, keeping us stuck in pain, making sure that we do not change. Fear begins as a little molehill, a small bump in the road of our lives. At that point all we need to do is put one toe into the fear and it will dissipate. Tomas calls it "walking through the fear." But when we choose not to deal with it, the fear grows from a little molehill into a large hill. It keeps growing and growing, and before we know it, we are faced with a mountain right at the center of our lives. We can no longer hide.

Our bodies become weary, our hearts anxious, yet we keep on going, tricking ourselves into believing that we are fine, that things are working out, that our life isn't really the way it appears to be. We convince ourselves that this is just temporary, that our situation will only be like this today, and that things will get better once another day emerges under the morning's sun. Until another day turns into another week, another week into another month, and another month into another year. And then the fear that paralyzed us has now become our friend. We know it is a destructive friend, but we are no longer disturbed by that thought for it no longer matters to us that fear is chipping away at the little that's left in our lives. Fear has become our comfort. It may not be the best of friends, but it is the only friend we are comfortable with, the only friend we have left—and we fear losing our so-called friend. We fear being without fear.

When I woke up from the hospital, I was told that everything went well but I wasn't sure because I was still in pain. At that time, doctors believed in total bed rest after surgery. For an entire year, I was not allowed to do any of the things I loved: tap dancing, ballet, or acrobatics. I went from being a very active child to a protected couch potato. It was like being stuck in a terrible nightmare. I felt I was being punished for getting sick. This was the beginning of my weight problem, which I've had to deal with all of my life.

After my health recuperated, my father often took me window-shopping in downtown Manhattan. I always looked forward to our trips together, as it was my special time with him alone. My father always held my hand when we were out together looking at all the stores. We would walk around, looking in the windows of the shops, talking, smiling, and enjoying each other's company. One day on our outing together, we stopped at one particular store. I was looking at all the fascinating things in the window and my father let go of my hand. When I turned around to talk with him, he was gone. I called and called for my father, but he did not respond. I searched for him, but I did not see him. A horrible panic came over me and I began to cry. After a few minutes, which felt like an eternity, my father came into view. His eyes were shining. He had a bright smile on his face. Father grabbed my hand and tried to calm me, saying that I was okay, that I was safe, that everything was all right. But I could not stop myself from crying and my body was shaking. Finally, Father said he would buy me anything I wanted in order for me to feel better. He did and I felt better. But then began my compulsive shopping addiction, as I learned through that experience that buying things was a way to get rid of my pain.

In my adult life, I've had visions of my father purposely letting go of my hand, hiding somewhere near but always keeping his eyes fixated on me. He would watch me, wait until I became alarmed, then rush to my side when I truly appeared distressed. Tomas has told me that my father was a man with very low self-esteem and in order for him to feel better about himself he enjoyed placing me in terrifying situations where he could easily "save" me. My father had never intended to hurt me. His only desire was to rescue me. Tomas explained that my father's self-esteem increased when he would end my state of distress, calming me down with the things he purchased for me. During these moments, Father felt most strong and powerful. It was as though he had gained heroic super powers.

However, from that day forth, I was never fully able to trust my father again. I no longer felt safe with him. I had the feeling that he might leave me alone again. This same scenario happened several more times, and I became severely afraid of going out with my father. I would feel so anxious, anticipating the moment he was going to let go of my hand, hoping I could hold on, wishing there was something I could do to prevent it from happening. My timing was always off. I could feel my father letting go but as soon as I turned around, he was nowhere to be found. Father loved to play this game. He was very good at it. He was fast, so fast. And I was too slow. But then came the day when the terror became unbearable for me. My body, mind, and soul couldn't take it anymore. Till this day I'm unsure of where I found the courage, but I went to my mother and begged her not to let my father take me out anymore. I never told her why.

Fear was created from the thought, "I am not enough." We worship with our beliefs and as we believe we aren't enough, we automatically become less than. Our beliefs become our truths. With the belief that we aren't enough, our truth becomes that we are in fact not enough, that there isn't enough and that we won't ever have enough. When we are in fear, we have a barrier separating us from trust and faith. We can't trust those we previously placed our faith in, we can't trust God, and worst of all, we can't trust ourselves. Just as trust and faith is the road leading to peace, the road leading to fear is always accompanied by the "what ifs" of the mind. But the question isn't whether we are afraid but rather if fear is a necessary part of life, and the answer to this question depends our perception, for fear by itself is neutral. Fear does not affect us. It cannot harm us. It has no power over us. None at all—unless of course, we feed into it.

We, as human beings, are here upon Mother Earth to learn, grow, and change. Our souls know this, our hearts know it, and so does our conscious mind. But our conscious mind, the small child, the ego, doesn't like this nor does it accept it as truth. Our conscious mind does not want to change. It wants everything to stay the same. It wants to be comfortable. Never mind that we are in intense pain. Never mind that our lives are collapsing around us. Never mind that we are still engaging in the same actions that have never worked out. Our conscious mind does not care about our wellbeing. It does not care that we are afraid, for it knows it can redirect us to be afraid of our fears. And when this doesn't work, there's always the option of being afraid of the fear of being fearful. Our conscious mind is a powerful dictator. It uses fear as its weapon to keep us right where it wants us to be: stuck, away from learning, growing, and changing.

But how do we get better? How do we move past such fear?

We walk through fear by doing the things we don't want to do. We walk through fear by doing the things that makes us uncomfortable. We walk through fear by confronting the things we are afraid of. The fearful mountain we have created in our lives is staring at us right in the face, reminding us of all the way we have failed to take responsibility for our lives. It is an outer symbol of our inner core belief. It is a symbol we have manifested to remind ourselves that we in fact aren't enough, that we do not have enough strength, courage, and willingness to move forward, that we are incapable of change. Ultimately, none of this is true. However, this is what we believe to be true about ourselves. And the only way to overcome this belief, the only way to move past this fear, is to place our hands over our ears, blocking out the negative phrases that have kept us stuck here so long. Quickly, we shut our eyes, and without thinking about it, we take a leap of faith and jump.

This is exactly what I did after meeting Tomas at the beach. I was still afraid but I had a great desire to understand what had happened to me. Though I desperately wanted to share my experience with someone, I did not tell anybody right away, fearing they would think I had lost my mind. The truth is, I thought I had lost my mind too. A few days later,

I called a close friend to see if she could help me make sense of my experience and maybe, just maybe, I could channel this Tomas. I'm not sure where I found the courage, but I ended up reaching out to my friend only to find out she was unavailable. However, I had taken the first leap of faith and jumped and I refused to turn back. I had a persistent feeling, pushing me to see if I could channel Tomas. "Why not?" I asked myself, fully aware of the shaking in my voice. I decided to take another leap of faith. I was going to try channeling this Tomas all by myself.

Before I knew it, I was rearranging the room, creating an atmosphere more conducive to channeling. I lit incense and had soft music playing on my stereo. I took out my old tape recorder and put in a blank cassette tape. I sat in a comfortable chair and closed my eyes. As I relaxed and followed my breath, I heard my voice chant, "Tomas. My most high guide, please come to me now." I had no idea where these words were coming from and I did not care. I was just chanting, over and over again. I remember feeling a sense of lightness and another feeling I hadn't quite experienced before. It was as if I had been placed in a trance. I was gone but my body was still here.

When I returned to realization from the trance, I immediately looked at the tape recorder. I had no idea how much time had passed, and I didn't even know if I had actually channeled Tomas. With anticipation, I rewound the tape. I was a little afraid, but over all excited to hear if anything had occurred.

As the tape replayed, I could hear the chanting of my voice. Then I heard myself stop chanting. I was now speaking in an unusual rhythm. "Your sister-in-law has made the decision to join your brother." This was all there was on the tape. I sat there, puzzled, while all kinds of emotions rippled through my body. My brother had died of lung cancer from second-hand smoke a year prior. I was unclear about the meaning of the recording on the tape. I gathered myself together and forced myself to replay the tape. I wanted to hear it again. I needed to hear it again. I heard it once more and I made the conscious decision to dismiss the message. Six months later, I got a phone call from my sister-in-law's sister, who informed me that my brother's wife had indeed passed away six months earlier.

Though I had chosen to dismiss the message, that same day I had also reached the point where I could no longer keep this to myself. The following day, I called another friend. I didn't care if she thought I was crazy. I just needed someone to listen. To my great surprise, my friend was very interested and immediately invited me to come over. When I arrived at her house, she encouraged me to channel so that she could talk with Tomas, the spirit guide. That evening, I again prepared myself to request Tomas to come forward. This time, it didn't take long for me to be removed from my body. I had no conscious memory of what happened or what was said but when I returned to my body, my friend told me that Tomas asked her to help me get used to him being in my body and speaking through me.

After a couple of evenings of channeling, I realized that my body had to acclimate to Tomas's high energy. I would get so energized that I became giddy, like having a whirling, dazed sensation. I also discovered that in order for Tomas to enter my body, he had to lower his energy and frequency level, while I had to raise my body's energy and frequency level to do the channeling. For a few months, we met every single night, and I channeled Tomas for my friend. At first, the sessions were short, but as I became more comfortable with the energy exchange, the sessions extended to a longer period of time. Eventually, I was able to better harmonize my body's low energy with the high energy of Tomas. We were finally in sync.

People often misunderstand the concept of being a channel. I am a trance channel, and that is relatively rare. Most people that channel are conscious; they are present in their body and do not give up control of their body to their spiritual guides. They are the ones speaking directly to other people, such as their clients, giving them messages and information from Spirit. I, on the other hand, do it differently. I close my eyes, go into a trance, and ask my guide to come forward. My clients speak directly to Tomas and receive the information from him—not from me. Generally, I am not aware of the information that has been given.

When I started channeling, I barely talked

with the people who came for their sessions with Tomas. Besides the necessary introductions, I did not address anyone, as I did not know what to say or do with them. These people were here to talk with Tomas, my spiritual guide. Not to me. I took no responsibility for the session or the information given, and I preferred it that way. I was afraid. So afraid that I would leave my body as quickly as possible. In fact, I could not get out of my body fast enough, gladly turning the meeting over to Tomas. From my point of view, what went on between the client and Tomas had nothing to do with me. When I would return to my body, I had no recollection of what occurred during the time I was gone. I had no conscious memory of the session other than what the client wanted to share with me. I was totally dependent on the person to tell me what happened during the session. At the time, I did not know what conscious channeling was. And to be quite honest, even if I had known, I would have wanted nothing to do with it. Having a spirit being come into my body to communicate to other human beings and give them information about their lives was fearful enough. I couldn't handle anything more.

Tomas never seemed to give me the option to consciously channel, and this was perfectly fine with me. I did not want to be looked upon as different. I wanted to be normal. I wanted to be just like everyone else, and I wanted to be liked by everyone else. I was terrified of being seeing as a strange person. I did not want to be associated with being weird or a freak.

It wasn't until much later when I became more comfortable with Tomas and that I also worked through my own lessons of trust and faith that I began to open up to the idea that people were genuinely curious about Tomas and me. Perhaps the most difficult concept that some people are unable to grasp is that my spiritual guide and I are not integrated. Tomas and I are two separate beings housed in one physical body (only when I'm channeling). He is his own being, with his own personality and character. I am my own being, with my own distinct personality and character. God created us both, just like everyone else. The only difference is that I am currently living in a human body upon Mother Earth while Tomas lives in the realm of Spirit and does not have a body.

Many have asked me how Tomas accesses information. Tomas has informed me that he is in direct contact with each person's guides and angels. In the Spirit world, we are all one. And in our oneness, there is an inner connection and recognition that all spirit beings have for each other and for us. As Pierre Teilhard de Chardin said, "We are not human beings having a spiritual experience. We are spiritual beings having a human experience." We are one. We are the same. At the beginning of a session, the first things Tomas says to a client is that he is from the Light and works for the Father in Heaven, the Source of all, God. He also says that he is unable to tell an untruth. This immediately calms people, as they feel more relaxed about talking to a being in spirit form. Tomas always asks each person for permission and nothing is ever done without his or her consent. He usually asks if the individual will allow him to look into their eyes. The eyes are the windows to the soul, and when Tomas gazes into a person's eyes, he receives information from that person's guides and angels. Tomas then delivers the information he has received in order to assist the person in their healing.

Our guides and angels are continually communicating with us. Sometimes we choose to hear them, and other times we don't. Most of the time, however, we are too busy listening to our small child mind, the ego, that we unconsciously choose not to hear the messages our guides and angels are telling us. There are times when we do hear the messages and consciously choose to ignore them. Tomas comes into the picture when your guides and angels enlist him to help them deliver their messages to you. Many people who have come for a session are shocked that they would be doing such a thing. They have no idea why they have come. But when they leave, they know.

I'm frequently asked where I go when Tomas comes into my body. Tomas has told me that I go to another dimension to learn valuable lessons. This is all he'll say about it. In rare instances, I have been brought back during a session between Tomas and a client when Tomas felt it was something I needed to witness. It is similar to a near-death experience. I am out of my body, looking down and seeing everything that is happening. It's like watching a movie, seeing it, but not being part of it. When this occurs, I am able to remember what took place during the session when I return to my body. These incidences occur only when there are lessons that I as well as the client need to learn simultaneously. Therefore it was for my growth and benefit to be present.

It has been over twenty-five years since I met Tomas. I can still tap into how I felt waking up the day after my forty-seventh birthday, stuck with my depressed thoughts, heading to the beach, relaxing, walking into the crystal room, THE THREE talking to me, and Tomas appearing. I always smile when I think about it. I can remember everything. It's all so crystal clear. But what I can't recall is the day my great fear of this experience vanished. A part of me believes my fear disappeared when I made the first step and called my friend, another part of me believes it was when I decided to channel Tomas alone. I realize it's not important that I don't remember the exact moment I was no longer terrorized by fear. What matters is that once I jumped, the fear disappeared long before I noticed it was gone.

"When we are in fear, we have a barrier separating us from trust and faith. Trust and faith is reserved for God and God alone, for God is the Source. The Source of All."

CHAPTER 3

THE SOURCE OF ALL

I HAD AN image of God. He was a tall, gigantic man, sitting on his enormous golden throne. I was the size of an ant, my feeble legs trembling as I walked forward to hear my judgment. In this giant god's left hand was a golden spear, at the tip, a laser, brighter than the sun's light. This laser had a defined purpose: to wipe away my existence from Earth. A punishment for my wrongdoings. Giant God's right hand held no weapon, yet it was more terrifying than his left. I watched him open his large right hand, stretching out his long fingers. He pointed his index finger right at me, and with a deep, deep voice, he said, "Today's the day! I'm gonna get you! I'm gonna get you! I'm gonna get you!"

This was my perception of God.

Tomas says when we are in fear, we have a barrier separating us from trust and faith. Who are we supposed to trust? I asked him. Who are we supposed to place our faith in? He responded by saying that trust and faith is reserved for God and God alone, for God is the Source. The Source of All. We have been conditioned to depend on things that are outside of us and rely on people that don't comprehend us. To place faith in anything other than God is to place faith in the unreal. We look at the creation, a reflection of the Creator, and are so amazed by His work that we fall in love. And rightfully so! Looking at God's creation regenerates us. It connects us to a forgotten place within ourselves where a passionate flame burns vibrantly. Staring into this flame makes us feel whole. It makes us feel safe. It makes us feel loved. Within the bat of an eye, we are obsessed. We worship the creation above the Creator, forgetting that the creation did not create itself. That it isn't the source of our joy, the fire that sustains us, the breath that gives us life.

It's a mistake we too often make. The creation is not the Creator. The creation is not God. People will disappoint us one way or another. Not because they are bad. Not because they are wrong. Not because they are evil. People disappoint for the simple reason that they are human. In their human condition, people are incapable of meeting our expectations twenty-four hours of each and every day of the week. Only God can do this! Yet we blame others when they hurt us, when they walk away from us, when they fail to be here for us in the exact way we expected them to be. "I trusted you," we are so accustomed to saying, "I placed my faith in you. And now I'll never trust anyone ever again."

But did we really trust this person? Did we really place our faith in them? Did we really expect them to be here for us in the exact way we believed they needed to be? We have not always been able to trust ourselves nor have we always believed in who we were. If we had trusted and believed in ourselves, we would have had no need to place our trust and faith in anything or anyone that is outside of us. We most certainly have not always been there for ourselves in the exact way we believed we needed to be. If for just one second, we step out of our small child mind, our ego, we would see that it was us who failed us and not those whom we'd pretended to have trusted. How did we come to the determination that we had the right to uphold other people to standards that we, ourselves, have been unable to meet?

When Tomas told me that trust and faith is reserved for God and God alone, I immediately wondered how in the world was I supposed to trust God when I wasn't sure who or what God was. The very idea of having to trust God sent jolts of panic throughout all the cells in my body. To make matters worse, how do I even fantasize about the idea of trusting God when my perception of God was one of fear, judgment, and punishment? How do I trust God when I believed He was just watching my every step, impatiently waiting around the corner for me to mess up so that He could snatch me in the middle of the night and condemn me to eternal hell?

In many holy books, it is written that God is love and that He is accepting, forgiving, and understanding. Flip the pages of the same holy books and you'll notice that the same God is also described as jealous, vengeful, and punitive. He has given us free will to do as we please but has also provided us a set of rules to live by. God-forbid we deviate from these rules. Flip more pages and you'll notice we are quickly reminded that we'll have to answer for our disobedience. Judgment day will come, they say. You'll have to answer for your sins, they say. You'll burn in hell, they say. Time and time again, the attributes of God fluctuate from love to hate and hate to love.

Who and what is God?

Tomas says God is AWESOME. He is beyond any human explanation. To describe all the attributes of God would take eternity and beyond. But I can tell you what God is not. He isn't fearful, judgmental, vengeful, or punitive. He isn't waiting around the corner to snatch us away. He isn't keeping a detailed list of our shortcomings, a list of all of our sins. Contrary to popular belief, God has no intention of condemning us to burn in eternal hell. This is perhaps one of the most hateful illusions we have created in our minds. Nothing about it is true. God does not hate us or seek to punish us when we fail. In fact, in God's eyes, we never fail. He loves us unconditionally. This means, no matter what we do, no matter what we do not do, God loves us and His love for us is forever constant. God's love does not increase when we do the things we label as "good" nor does it decrease when we partake in activities we label as "bad." God doesn't just love us. He is LOVE. And every time we love, we are one with God. When we allow love to flow through our hearts, our bodies, our beings, we are one with God and God is one with us. We aren't just loved. We are LOVE.

God's unconditional love is given freely to all of His creations at the exact moment of creation. We see it in the rising and setting of the sun, in the waves of the sea rolling forward and backward, eternally going on and on. We hear God's unconditional love in the whispering of the wind, the singing of birds, the rippling of rivers, the echoes of thunder. Place your hand upon your chest. Feel your heart beating inside of you. It's alive. You're alive. This is God's unconditional love. Now feel the palm of your hand resting softly against your chest, feel the breath moving from your nose, through your throat, into your lungs, reaching your belly, and out again it goes. This is God's unconditional love. It is anywhere and everywhere. It is here and there, anytime and all of the times.

There is a belief upon Mother Earth that we must work very hard and do the right things so that we may be worthy of God's love. This doesn't even come close to being the truth. There is nothing we must do in order to earn God's love. Nor can we

do anything to rid ourselves of it. God's unconditional love is our heritage and birthright. It is our
essence, our energy, our power. God's love is everything. This love is strongly rooted deep inside of
us. It is the eternal force that has guided us since
the moment of creation and will continue to guide
us throughout infinity and beyond. We receive
God's love simply because we are His beloved creations. And God's love sustains us simply because
we are. God's unconditional love is the All in All. It
is the All and All. There is nothing greater.

God is known by many names: Adonai, Allah,
El Elyon, El Shaddai, Jehovah, Lord, Yahweh,
and many more. God is also called Father, Mother,
Brother, Sister, Friend, He, She, It. Sometimes God
is referred to as Light, Source, Energy, Sustainer,
Creator, Higher Power, Universe. The name by
which we call God does not matter. What's important is to know that God is the Ultimate Creator,
the Source of All. It is also important to know as
the creations of this Creator, we are here to be an
expression of His power, His energy, and His love,
for that is our Father's essence. And that is the
essence in which He has created us to be. God is
love and so are we. In loving God, ourselves, our
brothers, our sisters, and every form of life, we
honor God, we honor ourselves, we honor love.

Who can love us like God? Who is able to create
us like God? Who knows us like God?

No one. No one at all. In remembrance of
this truth, we can now laugh at ourselves—not in

judgment, but in love, for we have now come to the realization that only God and God alone is deserving of our total trust and faith. God is our most trusted friend. He is the one to whom we confide our darkest secrets. He sees us just as we are, and he accepts us as we are. God is everything we have searched for. He is everything we have ever wanted, everything we have ever needed. What a blessing it is to know that we were made by something so great, so powerful, so magnificent. What a blessing it is to know that we are eternally connected to this Light, this Energy, this Source of All. What a blessing it is to know that we can place our trust and faith in God, knowing He loves us no matter what.

How do we trust God?

We do so by loving Him, by accepting His will for us. God's will is that we be happy, joyous, and free, and most importantly that we learn to love ourselves in the same capability that He loves us—unconditionally. I wish I could tell you that loving yourself unconditionally was the easiest thing you would ever do. It isn't. In fact, it's the most difficult thing you'll ever do. Loving yourself unconditionally takes a lot of patience, strength, and willingness. It isn't easy to see all of your qualities and flaws revealed to you. Loving yourself unconditionally is a lifelong journey. Tomas often tells me the spiritual meaning of love is acceptance. As human beings, we are addicted to guilt, shame, regret, and punishment—all are blocks of judgment preventing us from accepting ourselves. They prevent us from loving ourselves. There is only one way to trust God. There is only one way to demonstrate our faith in Him. We must let go of our will and accept His will. We must let go of our conditional love and accept His unconditional love.

"Acceptance is to give up the fight and accept the reality of what is. Whether we like it or not, we get exactly what we need at the exact moment we need it to move forward in our lives."

CHAPTER 4

THE WALL OF JUDGMENT

SOME MOMENTS ARE a grain of sand in the desert, a drop of rain in the sea, a gush of wind in a storm. They are minuscule, but they have profound effects. These moments are the fraction of the second that exists right before dawn turns into morning and day into night. They are the moments between which we experience the farewell of one season and the welcome of another. The importance of these liminal moments cannot be undermined. They are catalytic. They carry with them the power to change things. However small they may be, these moments cannot be measured or confined into space. In fact, they move through us with such enormous force that when we experience them, we know without a doubt we are no longer the same and that we can never again be the same as before. We are transformed. We are forever changed.

I have learned many lessons throughout my spiritual journey. I have learned small things. I have learned big things. I have learned lessons that I only needed to practice for a day and other lessons that I have practiced for weeks, months, and several years. The ability to remain open is one of the most important lessons I have learned. Being flexible with my thoughts, beliefs, and actions has helped tremendously with my growth. There will never come a time when we will stop learning. Life simply does not work this way. A great part of being alive is about growing and changing. We grow and change through the lessons we learn. Learning can sometimes feel overwhelming. This is why it's important to know that we don't have to master everything at the exact moment the lessons are taught to us. The key is to remain open and to do the best that we can do. Lessons are always simple; although sometimes they feel difficult, they are simple spiritual truths that transform us into better human beings when we allow it. Our Father in heaven does not force anything upon us. God only provides the experiences through which we learn. Whether or not we learn is up to us.

My heart's greatest desire is to be the person God wants me to be, and I must admit that more often than not, I have no idea what that looks like. But I trust in God's process. And day by day, I notice the many ways in which I have grown. There is a misconception that walking the path of spirituality is about reaching for perfection. This simply isn't true. Everyone is on a spiritual path, whether or not they are aware of it. And walking the path of spirituality has nothing to do with perfection. Improvement is what it's all about. Perfection is reserved for God. As human beings, we are only perfect in our imperfections. To expect anything else is to set a trap for unrealistic expectations. When we are unable to achieve the expectations we hold dear, we become extremely disappointed in ourselves. And the disappointment we feel is usually followed by much anger and resentment towards our own self.

I have learned from Tomas that whatever you believe will become your truth—even if it isn't the ultimate truth. If you believe you are loved, you will feel loved and your life will be an expression of love. You will experience peace, joy, love, and empowerment. Your heart will overflow with gratitude as you realize that love is the motivator behind every step you take, every decision you make. You will be in awe of the blessings that are constantly manifesting in your life. You will see the positive in everything that surrounds you. You will know peace, the peace of God. And in knowing peace, you will know God. In knowing God, you will have also come to know yourself, for the way to God is the way to self.

On the other hand, if you believe you are cursed, you will feel cursed and your life will be a reflection of dreadful experiences that will reaffirm to you that your core belief and your truth is that you are indeed cursed. You will survive one horrid experience only to be faced with ten more. You'll be angry, anxious, and fearful as you fight your situation, your life, your world. Nothing will ever be good enough. Life as you know it will not only feel like hell on Earth, it will *be* hell on Earth. And then will come the day when you'll curse everything that surrounds you. But first you'll curse yourself, and through that action, you will have also cursed your Creator, for what we give to ourselves, we directly give to God.

Another simple nevertheless important lesson I have learned from Tomas is that judgment is rooted in core belief. And that core belief is self-esteem. Core belief is the mirror showing us the things we believe about ourselves. Whether we like or dislike them, love or hate them, these parts of ourselves are constantly being reflected back to us. Whether they are true or untrue and whether we accept or reject them, these parts of ourselves make up who we are. The core-belief mirror also shows us exactly how we feel about ourselves, which in fact is our self-esteem. We believe the things that are being shown to us because we feel them. And as we feel them, our beliefs about these parts of ourselves grows with greater strength and power.

Our beliefs are deeply intertwined inside of us. Like the roots of a tree, they reach all the way down to the core of our beings. Our lives are a direct reflection of our core beliefs, which are the motivator behind the choices we make. We aren't always aware of this truth; nonetheless, our core beliefs are the motor driving us forward or backward. A tree isn't strong or weak because of its trunk, its branches, its leaves, or the fruits it bears. These things are just a mere reflection of its roots. This isn't to say that the trunk of the tree, the branches, the leaves, or the fruits are any less important. They are valuable parts of the tree because these are the parts that are visible to the human eye. One cannot gaze through the soil to see what's going on down in the roots of the tree. But one can take a look at the trunk, the branches, the leaves, and the fruits to determine whether or not the roots of the tree are healthy and strong. It is the roots that keep the tree grounded so that its branches may flow in the circle of life. It is the same for us.

I was one of these people who truly believed I was cursed. I would spend hours, sometimes days, self-loathing and miserable about all the ways in which my life was bad. And believe me, it was bad. In fact, life as I knew it was awful. It was hell. If ever I was asked to state the things I hated about my life, I quickly jumped to the occasion, verbalizing an endless list: there was my food addiction, my shopping addition, my addiction to debt, and last but not least, my addiction to my addictions. I could go on and on, from top to bottom, and inside and out, listing all of the things I hated about myself. However, if I was asked to speak of the things I loved about my life I needed a minute to think about it. In truth, I needed several minutes to think everything through. When I finally managed to list one thing, I quickly shut down as I realized that I didn't really love the thing I was saying. I didn't even truly like it. I somewhat liked it. And after stating the thing I somewhat liked about my life, I immediately needed to pause for another moment in order gather my thoughts and come up with another thing I might somewhat like.

I was well into my fifties when I started to remember little eight-year-old Helenne and her father. As a child, I barely got to spend time with my beloved hero. Father belonged to the restaurant industry where he worked as a waiter. He was the sole provider for the family, and it was quite usual for him to work anywhere from sixty to eighty hours per week. Father would come home late in the night or sometimes early in the morning, an hour or two before sunrise. He was usually tired, drained, and downright exhausted. My father seldom had time to talk or play with me. But on the rare occasions when we did spend time together, my favorite thing to do was to lay on a pillow across his lap as he rubbed my back. I loved it when Father did that! The feeling of his palm running against my back was soothing. It made me feel warm and fuzzy inside. It made me feel important in his eyes, like I was a valuable part of his life. It made me feel loved. Every time Father rubbed my back, I felt that I had finally mattered.

The way my father treated me was very much different than the way my mother reacted towards me. When spending time with Father, I wasn't the bad thing Mother wanted nothing to do with. I wasn't the wrong thing she needed to chase away. I wasn't the good-for-nothing thing that could never live up to her expectations. Father never compared me to my brother the way Mother did. In fact, when I grew up into my late teenage years, I got to see that I was my father's favorite. As a little girl growing up alongside my father, I was able to be myself as much as I knew what being myself was about. It was just him and me. I was little Helenne, his beloved daughter, and he was the hero who rescued me from Mother's rage. Father made me feel welcomed. The same way one feels when coming to a happy, well-put-together home. It was like arriving at a safe place, a loving place. I would close my eyes, smiling internally while enjoying the attention he was giving me. Father knew how to make me feel good.

Good always feels good until it does not.

The good feelings came at a steep price. It was a price my eight-year-old self gladly paid so that she could feel loved in her father's eyes, not having anyone else to make her feel loved, not having anywhere else where she could receive love. The memories zipped forward, or in this case, they flashed back, and within a matter of seconds, I saw little eight-year-old Helenne tickling her girly innocence with her father's maturity. For a moment I stepped back in time as forgotten memories from decades ago resurrected inside of me. I could feel everything. My eight-year-old self wasn't afraid. She was comfortable. This was very familiar to her, because she and her father had done this many times before. It was their feeling-good activity. It was how her father showed her love. And little Helenne had wanted to feel loved more than anything in the world. She had needed to feel loved.

In an instant, I was brought back to the present, where good did not feel good anymore. As an adult I knew how sickening what I had seen had been. My entire body shook in terror. My eyes rolled around madly as my head shook from side to side. There was a loud sound pounding at my temples. It made my head ache. It all felt so heavy. The remembrance enveloped me with three additional layers of skin: guilt, shame, and regret. These negative feelings weren't new to me. We'd coexisted most of my life. But they were always dormant, sleeping somewhere deep inside of me. They left me with just enough energy to exist but not to live. Living was for the healthy. Living was for the good. Living was for the clean, the pure, the holy, the innocent. Little Helenne wasn't any of these things. And so she pushed down her guilt, shame, and regret—not wanting to feel, not wanting to remember.

But now these feelings had awakened. They were right in my face, right in my consciousness. And I feared they were here to stay. I quickly shut my eyes, hoping that all of it would fade into oblivion. I wiped the tear falling down my quivering cheeks. It was at this very moment that a small voice in my mind whispered to me. "You were enjoying it," it said casually, as if we were longtime friends. "You liked it. Didn't you?" I searched my confused brain for a response. I needed to say something. I needed to explain to the voice that I wasn't...that I didn't...that I couldn't... I couldn't... I couldn't... I couldn't breathe. The air was being expunged from my lungs. My body buckled the way a fish does when it is removed from water. My heart stopped beating. I crumbled down on the floor, burying my face in my hands as the core of my being shattered inside of me. I was broken. Broken into a million pieces. And when the million pieces cracked, each piece shattered into a million more.

I wasn't sure I'd survive.

Human beings make a habit of saying they don't know how they'll survive, and I'm no exception to the rule. We say this not because the words feel good upon our lips but because the pain we feel is unbearable. The pain is so excruciating that we truly believe that we don't know how we'll survive, if we'll survive. This is what we believe down in the core of whatever's left in our being. This is our truth. The memories replayed across my mind like a never-ending nightmare. And I got to see over and over again the shameful things my father and I did when I was a little girl. Each new time I saw it, became more painful than the last. I wanted it to stop. I wanted the memories to go away. I wanted them to leave me alone. I could feel the uneasiness crawling under my eight-year-old skin, like a foreign organism that desired to be there but knew it did not belong. A part of me must have known that something was off. But there was also another part of me that was well aware that my body liked the pleasurable sensations it was experiencing. And that's the part I was most ashamed of.

As an adult, the whole thing was immensely confusing to me. Here I was on the outside, looking in, feeling immeasurably guilty. It's not the guilt you feel when your parents say you ought to be ashamed for sneaking out of your room during the middle of the night, tiptoeing around the kitchen as you steal your favorite snack out of the cookie jar. It's not the type of guilt you feel when you lie to your parents, telling them you were sorry, knowing very well that you weren't. No!!! The guilt I felt had no comparison. I was deeply ashamed and regretful. I felt bad. I felt wrong. I felt dirty. If I had the power to go back in time and reverse the clock, I would have done so in a heartbeat. But such powers were out of my reach, and I was left to deal with this ugly reality that I wanted nothing to do with. I prayed for it to go away. But no matter how much I prayed, my reality remained ever present in my life. Even when I closed my eyes, I could feel my reality staring right back at me. I could almost reach forward and touch it.

Accepting others and ourselves is easy when we feel safe and secure within our beings. But when our comfort is disturbed and our sense of security vanishes, the notion of acceptance seems out of reach, impossible even. Both of my parents had already passed away when my childhood memories surfaced, yet I found myself becoming very angry with them. Being angry with anybody is tiresome enough, but being angry with the dead, well, that's a draining process. It sucked whatever energy I had left. It wasn't like I could have gone to the cemetery and knocked on my parents' tomb and said, "Hey Mom, Dad, I'd like to discuss my childhood with you." I suppose I could have stormed out of my condo, gotten in the car, and driven over a hundred and twenty miles per hour as I made my way to the cemetery to lash out my anger. It was by the grace of God that I had just enough clarity in my fifties to realize that doing such a thing wasn't going to get me anywhere. I had no family members to turn to, no friend I felt I could share this experience with. No one to understand the hurdles I was facing. It was just me, all alone, broken, incomplete, my disturbing memories and feelings keeping me company.

I was upset with my father for what he had done and even more so with my mother for what she had not done. In some of the memories, I saw my mother glancing over her shoulder, looking at my father and me. She saw what was happening between the two of us, and after a few seconds she twisted her neck to look the other way. As time passed by, my anger towards my mother escalated out of control. It was like riding a rollercoaster, where I became angrier and angrier the higher I went. This level of anger troubled me greatly, but I didn't know how to even begin to calm myself. Some say forgive and forget. And that is a beautiful phrase when we are able to do it. But when we can't get ourselves to forgive, when we can't can snap a finger and forget, that phrase becomes one of the most irritating sentences to have been invented. I couldn't help but feel that my anger towards my mother was justified, like I had the right to be angry with her. She was my mother. She'd witnessed what happened. And she chose to ignore what she had seen with her own two eyes. I couldn't understand nor did I have compassion for the way she had behaved.

The most troubling part about my anger was the knowledge that I wasn't as nearly angry with my parents as I was with myself. The shame of seeing my father and me this way made me believe that I was deserving of all the pain and suffering I had endured throughout my life. Little Helenne had been so bad. She had been so wrong. A part of her had enjoyed the abuse that had been inflicted on her. And in my eyes, that made her guilty. It made her part of the problem. There was a part of my younger self that had liked being with my father in this way. I am well aware that I hadn't been fully comfortable with it. A part of little Helenne had known that something was off. This is where I birthed my guilt. And this is where my shame overwhelmed me. I often wonder how long ago this belief had been instilled inside of me. I have wondered if this was the very reason why my younger self had believed that she'd deserved to be judged. That she'd deserved to be punished. And judged and punished, she was!

Tomas says judgment comes from control and control comes directly from expectations. By remembering my childhood abuse, I got to see that my expectations of my father, my mother, and myself had failed me miserably. I always knew I did not have a healthy childhood. But I wasn't aware of the extent of the dysfunction and its impact on my life. I got engaged twice. And each time, I was the one who ended the engagement. I couldn't trust men. I couldn't trust myself. I couldn't trust God. My entire childhood, as I previously believed it, was a lie. A big fat lie. And to deepen the wound, there was nothing pretty about the truth I had been left with. From my point of view, the truth of my child-hood was nasty and dirty. It was awful. I didn't like it and I refused to accept it.

I fought as hard as I could, sometimes as hard as I couldn't. I fought with everything I had and everything I did not have. I fought and fought and fought not to accept the reality I had been left with. The fighting was helpless. It only made things worse. I became even more drained of energy. I constantly felt weary and more lost than ever before. Yet I continued to fight as my real-ity refused to transform into the pretty picture I wanted it to be. I needed to achieve my goal of a beautiful life, and my childhood was in the way.

It had happened in the past, sure, I knew. But at the time, it was a very real part of my present and it was affecting my future. I had a great desire to achieve this expectation of a beautiful life. I wanted a life where I could feel whole and complete. I wanted to wipe out my past and start over again. I wanted a clean state, so that I could feel worthy, so that I could feel loved. I had never wanted to accomplish anything so badly. I craved this reality as much as the desert craves water, as much as a newborn craves their mother's touch. I kept on fighting to create this reality for myself. But the problem was, I never asked God for help. I wanted to do it my way. When I came to the realization that I wouldn't achieve my expectations for the life I wanted in the way I wanted it, I became extremely disappointed in myself. And I judged myself to be a failure.

Judgment is the wall separating us from the path to acceptance. This wall is built with heavy blocks of painful childhood experiences that over the years have been coated with layers upon layers of experiences that brought us guilt, shame, and regret. Judgment was created by us through us. It came out of our imperfect human need to label our experiences. Everything that we judge is based on our perception. And perception is unique to each individual. Perception is founded on each person's distinct life experiences. No two humans have ever had or will ever have the same life experiences. And even if they did, they would never perceive their experiences in the exact manner.

In our humanness, we have chosen not to perceive our experiences for what they are—experiences. In attempting to process what happens to us, we have chosen to attach a label to our experiences based on the way they make us feel. This is the beginning of our journey towards the wall of judgment. This is the beginning of us making ourselves less than. This is the beginning of self-punishment and self-sabotage. This the beginning of getting ourselves in major trouble. This is the beginning of punishing ourselves for our failures. We judge ourselves to be less than we really are. Then we get scared that someone will see through our façade and see who we really are. This isn't our fault. We weren't born this way. We didn't set out to be judgmental. This is something we have learned. We have learned to judge from those closest to us, those we trust. And they as well have learned to judge from those they were closest to, those they trusted.

There are six terms of judgment: good, bad, right, wrong, should, and I don't know.

Was it good or bad that memories forgotten decades ago found their way back into my life? Was it right or wrong that once these memories surfaced, my image of my dad as my childhood hero turned into one of a villain? Should my mother have done something about what she witnessed?

Should I have felt the way I did? Good, bad, right, and wrong are the leading words in our phrases when we question ourselves in judgment. We consistently wonder if we were good or bad, right or wrong. If the things we experienced were the good and right things, or if they were bad and wrong. We ask ourselves if they were the things we should have experienced or the things we should have avoided.

But ultimately, who decides what's good or bad? Right or wrong? What should or shouldn't occur? Who is qualified to make such a determination? And under what requirement does he or she determine if there is in fact something or someone that needs to be judged? And if there is indeed a need to judge, how then, do we determine the appropriate judgment? Who among us is qualified to cast the first stone?

We are all imperfect human beings. We have no right to judge others. We have no right to judge ourselves, for the Ultimate Creator, the Source of All, God, has never and will never judge us. An experience is an experience. It isn't good. It isn't bad. It isn't right. It isn't wrong. The experience, however, may feel good. It may feel bad. It may feel right. It may feel wrong. But that does not mean it is any of these things. The way we feel towards our experiences is just that—the way we feel. But the experience itself is neutral. It just is.

There are no "shoulds."

No one is an expert in determining whether

something should or shouldn't have occurred. To "should" upon a situation, an experience, or a person is to be in severe judgment as none of us are in control. God is in control of everything that moves under the sun. He is the only one to be in control of everything that exists. God is the only controller of everything that happens in the universe. The sun does not look to us for permission to rise or set. Nor does the Earth ask for our opinion on its rotation and revolution. They look to God, their Creator. Though we may not always understand why certain things happen the way they do, it isn't our place to be resentful, believing something or someone should or should not have been the way it was. Everything is always the way it needs to be.

When we are not busy labeling our experiences as good, bad, right, or wrong, we are preoccupied with saying, "I don't know." Boy, do we love to say I don't know! I don't know what's going on with me. I don't know why I'm the way I am. I don't know why I'm sad. I don't know why I'm angry. I don't know why I feel this way. We are obsessed with the notion of "I don't know." We say this perhaps because we believe we do not know or perhaps because not knowing feels true to us. But make no mistake. The notion of "I don't know" is a lie, and it's a judgment we place upon our situations, our experiences, and ourselves.

Deep inside of us, we have all knowledge. God always knows; therefore, we always know. We are one with God. To say we do not know is to say God doesn't know—which isn't true. What we choose to do is not to know. We choose to deny our truths. We choose to deny our knowing. To choose not to know a thing does not make the thing unknowable.

When we are in judgment, we judge our situations, our experiences, our feelings, our actions, our beliefs. We judge ourselves. We judge others. We judge God. When we are in judgment, we are in fear and we allow fear to drive us to come up with ways to punish ourselves. We allow fear to control our lives. We allow fear to be our god. We surrender anything and everything over the god of fear that we have created. We devote our lives to this god of fear and we honor this god of fear by being ever more judgmental. When we are in judgment, we set unrealistic expectation for ourselves, and when we don't meet these expectations, we create a barometer to further judge ourselves as good, bad, right, or wrong. We punish ourselves with guilt, shame, regret, anger, depression, and anxiety. We punish ourselves with drama, chaos, and disease. We punish ourselves with many more unloving things as one of our unfortunate talents is to develop new ways of punishing ourselves. In punishing ourselves, we punish others, we punish God, and we punish every form of life. It's a never-ending cycle.

How do we break through the wall of judgment?

We do so by choosing to see through the eyes of God, the eyes of truth. It's not about liking or disliking the things we do or do not do, the things that have or have not happened to us, the things that we have or not have played a part of. Rather, it's about accepting things for what they are at this very moment. Acceptance is about letting go of our egocentric need to expect, control, judge, fight, or punish. Acceptance gives us the opportunity to lay down the sword we are piercing through our bleeding hearts. Acceptance gives us a chance to begin to heal. Acceptance teaches us how to love ourselves. Acceptance teaches us how to love others. Acceptance is the key.

The blessings that come along with acceptance are abundant and plentiful. They do not run out. There's always more. Acceptance is to give up the fight and accept the reality of what is. Whether we like it or not, we get exactly what we need at the exact moment we need it to move forward in our lives. Sometimes the exact experience we need is the one to bring us the most pain, but in order to accept our reality, we have to remove the labels we place upon our experiences. We have to learn to break through the wall of judgment and walk towards the path of acceptance. Forgiveness is the tool that helps us do just that.

"Peace is the gift of freedom: freedom from judgment, freedom from fear, freedom from illusion. When are free, we know what it means to be."

CHAPTER 5

THE PATH
TO ACCEPTANCE

THERE WAS A time in my life when I came to believe that God had given me a new brain. I don't mean that God, in His infinite power and wisdom, had changed my thoughts, intentions, and beliefs into what He wanted them to be, though these parts of myself had indeed changed. What I mean by God giving me a new brain is just that—I felt in my heart and believed in my soul that God had given me a new brain. This conviction left no fear dwelling inside of me. Just pure joy and excitement. These feelings were like bubbles of light that illuminated my senses. They left me with a high where I only felt better and better as time passed by. To top it all, there wasn't a brutal crash when my senses calmed down. It was a smooth venture. A most peaceful journey. I was amazed by the many wonders God had performed through me, for me, in me, and as me. My entire being overflowed with gratitude at the realization that God had transformed me.

Tomas says there is no forgiveness in the world of Spirit because everything in Spirit is seeing through the eyes of God, the eyes of truth, the eyes of love. The world of Spirit is the world of God. And in God's world, love is the only reality that exists. Where love is, God is, and where God is, all is in divine order. I'd be lying if I didn't tell you that something shook inside of me as soon as I heard that forgiveness did not exist. I struggled with the idea because it challenged one of my deepest child-hood beliefs. For as long as I could remember, I had been taught to seek forgiveness. I sought for-giveness from my parents and my friends, as well as other people. It was very difficult for me to hear that forgiveness wasn't real. Tomas had just told me that there is no forgiveness in God's world and that just didn't sit well with me, especially when I had been taught to ask for forgiveness from the divine forgiver: God, Himself.

In my mind, the words Tomas had spoken were like dark clouds assembling with one another in preparation for a coming storm. Clarity was not on the horizon. Or so I thought. As a child, I don't recall ever asking anyone about the purpose of forgiveness. But I do remember learning that I needed forgiveness because of my sins, mistakes, and shortcomings. I needed forgiveness when I had been bad, wrong, or less than what someone, usually my parents, needed me to be. Throughout my childhood, I also got to learn that forgiveness wasn't all about me. I was taught to ask for forgiveness for other people too. It became my responsibility to seek forgiveness for other's faults and errors as I learned from a very young age that other people's wellbeing came before my own. The benefits of forgiveness weren't fully explained to me. I was just told that it was something that I needed to do. And so when the time came, I dutifully asked for forgiveness and without protest, I forgave as well.

Prior to Tomas, it had never crossed my mind that the notion of forgiveness was a phantom idea. When you have learned something from childhood and practiced it into adulthood, that something automatically becomes second nature to you. It becomes a part of you—a real part. You don't ask yourself why you're doing it or how come you've always done it. You don't even question if the thing you are doing is truly what you believe or if it's something you've been conditioned to believe. You just do it. You do it the same way you've done it a thousand times before. You do it in the same manner you'll do it a thousand times more. Can you imagine the confusion that overpowered my mind when Tomas said there is no forgiveness in God's world? This isn't what I was taught. This isn't what I knew to be true. How in the world could this be? And how come I had never heard this before? What did it mean if it was actually true? How would this truth affect my life?

Thankfully, I have been blessed with a very patient spiritual guide. Tomas took his time to explain that forgiveness comes with two elements: victim and blame. If these two elements are absent, there is nothing to forgive. Love is the only reality Spirit knows. Love is the essence of everything God creates, for God is love. Things such as mistakes, wrongs, errors, victims, blame, and perpetrators are nonexistent in God's world. There are no accidents in life. Everything, and I mean everything, is simply a lesson to be learned.

We are constantly being presented with the opportunity to learn, grow, and change. In God's world, there are only lessons. These lessons challenge the countless souls who have chosen to enroll in the class of life. We are here upon Mother Earth because we chose to be. We signed a divine contract of our own free will to come and experience this life. We knew there would be lessons, as we were the ones who willingly signed up for these lessons. But before we were born into this human body, we went through a veil that wiped away our memory of making this voluntary choice.

The lessons we experience upon Mother Earth are often extremely difficult. They challenge us to rise above the illusion, which can very much appear real even though it is not. Learning through these experiences help us detach from the fear-based reality of this world in order to embrace the ultimate reality of God's world: love. In God's world, there are neither victims nor perpetuators, only lessons. This is the very reason why there is no forgiveness in God's world. Because in God's reality, nothing that warrants forgiveness has ever occurred.

Forgiveness is a gift that exists upon Mother Earth. It is the tool that helps us break through the wall of judgment and walk towards the path of acceptance. Forgiveness is a gift from us to us. There is a duality that exists in our world: hot and cold, short and tall, small and big. And forgiveness was created on Mother Earth as a gateway for those who desire to leave judgment behind in favor of the gift of acceptance. Tomas says forgiveness is reserved for self. Not anyone else. And he says this because it's not other people we are having a hard time forgiving. We find it difficult to forgive ourselves. To compensate for our own lack, we withhold, or trick, ourselves into believing that we are withholding forgiveness from others when truly we are denying ourselves.

I fought for a very long time, fought until I had no fight left in me before I came to the realization that I wasn't really fighting the things I thought I was fighting. I wasn't even fighting the people I thought I was fighting with. Nor the situations I believed I was fighting. For many years, I had been under the illusion that I was fighting a war of childhood abuse against my deceased parents, fighting against the reality I was stuck with, fighting against the world I'd become accustomed to. I even believed that I was fighting the good fight, the real fight, the true fight. But then came God. Through His loving grace and mercy, God removed the veil of trickery that had blinded me for far too long, allowing me to glare into the mirror of truth.

I, Helenne Deutscher, was fighting Helenne Deutscher. I was fighting the little girl who, through no fault of her own, had been abused in every imaginable way. I had spent all of my energy doing to her what I blamed my parents for doing to me. I had spent a great deal of time inflicting unto her the very hurtful things that had been inflicted unto me. There is a saying that the truth shall set you free. And yes, I felt free because I was now aware of the many unloving ways in which I had abused myself. The hurt that I caused to me was more painful than the hurt I experienced with my parents. But knowledge of this truth broke the little strength I had left in my heart. How does one measure the guilt one feels when one realizes that she has played a major factor in her own self-destruction? I was no different than my parents. I gave little Helenne much pain and punishment. I gave her fear. I gave her lack. I gave her low self-esteem. I reinforced in the little girl that was still struggling to survive that her belief of not being good enough was the truth. Time and time again, by rejecting her, I reaffirmed to her that she was in fact not worth anything at all.

The pioneering psychologist, Carl Jung, is

credited for saying, "Until you make the unconscious conscious, it will direct your life and you will call it fate." I could not agree more. Throughout all of these years, I had never stopped to consider that maybe, just maybe, little Helenne had been through enough. That she had suffered enough, that she had been fearful enough, that she had been judged enough, that she had been punished enough. I had never before stopped to consider that my younger self had needed forgiveness, compassion, and acceptance. That for once in her life she had needed to be loved. In her book, *A Return to Love*, author and speaker Marianne Williamson wrote, "We are not held back by the love we didn't receive in the past, but by the love we're not extending in the present." It wasn't until my unconscious mind became conscious that I came to the realization that I had suffered tremendously from childhood into adulthood because I had refused to give to myself the love I desperately needed.

It hurt to know I was partly responsible for the life I had been left with. However, as painful as the truth may sometimes feel, nothing can replace the feeling of liberation one feels by coming face to face with it. Seeing the truth revealed to you is a powerful thing. It makes tears well from the eyes—tears of joy, tears of liberation, tears of love, tears of healing. The moment we come face to face with the truth, we are instantly empowered. Everything becomes so much clearer. The possibilities that appear on the horizon are endless. We have the power to make another choice. We have the power to change our course. We have the power to heal the wounds we have bled from. We have the power to transform into everything we've always dreamed of. And best of all, we aren't alone in our journey of transformation. We don't do this by ourselves. We do it with God.

By lifting the veil of trickery, God gave me a gift—a priceless gift. God's gift to me was the opportunity to see this entire situation in His truth and to give up the fight if I chose to do so. God was literally handing me a box of healing, and it was entirely up to me to accept it. But to accept God's gift, I first needed to feel deserving of it. And to feel deserving of such a gift, I needed to come to a point where I had had enough pain, punishment, judgment, suffering, and misery. I needed to make the conscious decision that I, Helenne Deutscher, was worthy of more. God's love was what I needed to believe I was worthy of. And thank God, by that point, I had become a devoted believer.

I now know in my heart that my parents had never meant to hurt me. I know this because God revealed it to me. My parents loved me. They loved me not in the way I needed to be loved but in the way they knew how to love. They were disturbed individuals whose idea of love was born of pain and demonstrated through abuse. My parents had never learned about a love born of kindness, patience, compassion, acceptance, and understanding. Pain was the love that had been taught to them.

It was the love they believed in. It was the love that was their truth. My parents had been deeply hurt by the people they were closest to. These people had claimed to love my parents and demonstrated their love to them by inflicting pain, punishment, and abuse. This is how my parents came to believe down to the core of their being that love hurts. There is nothing about love that is painful. Love doesn't hurt at all. People do. Unfortunately, my parents had not gotten the memo.

I believe everything between my father and me started out innocently. As time passed by, my father lost himself and projected unto me the abuse that had been done to him. He had been molested and in turn molested me. This isn't to defend his actions. There is nothing to defend. As for my mother, she was completely financially dependent on my father. And I believe the pressure of standing up to my father, being left alone with a child, and not having any means by which to survive on her own was terribly terrifying to her. She chose to ignore what she had seen, not because she didn't love me, but because she was very much afraid. I also believe that my mother took out her rage on me because she hated the person she had become. I was the reminder of the pain she couldn't escape from, the reminder that she had failed to achieve her motherly expectations of herself. In abusing me, she got to punish herself over and over again. She used me as the mirror to punish herself because it's what she believed she deserved.

It's not my place to judge my parents. I'm just grateful that God has given me the clarity I needed in order to understand that my parents were broken people who in turn broke me. Because that's what broken people do. They break others. I do not wish for anyone to experience the pain I went through. If I had the power to spare anyone from the childhood abuse I had to endure, I would do it in a heartbeat. But such things are out of my control. Somewhere deep inside of me is the knowledge that my childhood experiences were crucial in my learning to stop judging myself. Perhaps I could I have learned this in a less painful way. But God had me learn it this way. I don't need to ask "why?" or "how come?" because I've learned to trust in God's plan for me. This was the way I needed to learn in order to be of service to myself, God, and others. Surviving my childhood experiences has led me on the path of learning about kindness, compassion, acceptance, and love for myself as well as others who need it most. These experiences, as painful as they were, have made me stronger, wiser, better. They have taught me about the unlimited healing power of God. My parents were my master teachers. I do not like what they did to me, but I'm grateful that today I can say God has healed the wounds they inflicted upon me as well as the ones I inflicted upon myself. Today as I am writing this, I am still amazed by the healing power of God. It's a grandiose topic deserving of a book of its own.

It took a while for me to come to terms with the role I played in the abuse that occurred with my father. I carried a lot of guilt, shame, and regret about enjoying the sensations of the sexual abuse. I am most fortunate that Tomas has explained to me that the human body, like many other things, is neutral. The body simply reacts to whatever is being done to it. Had my father lit a match and burnt me with it, I would have been screaming from the pain. But my father did not inflict physical pain upon me. What he did was inflict pleasure. An eight-year-old child doesn't just come up with something like this. These things were taught to me by my father. I don't believe that he ever penetrated me. I never saw it in the memories nor do I feel it in my heart to be true. What I have seen is my father touching my body, making me feel good. Naturally, my body reacted to the pleasurable sensations. It isn't good, bad, right, or wrong. It has no "should" or "should not." My body simply reacted in the way it knew how.

In knowing this truth, I have made the conscious decision to lay down the invisible dagger I was stabbing little Helenne's heart with. I chose to stop judging myself for believing that I was bad, wrong, and dirty. I made the conscious choice to give to myself the gift of forgiveness. As previously stated, forgiveness is reserved for self. No one else. It is a gift from us to us. And as we give this gift to ourselves, we automatically give it to others. We are all worth forgiving because we are all children of God, created in love. The only requirement for us to extend forgiveness to ourselves is to believe we are worthy of it. I, Helenne Deutscher, am worthy of the gift of forgiveness for no other reason than the fact that I am a child of God. I know that God loves me no matter what. And I know this with certainty. Therefore, I chose to forgive myself for the guilt, shame, and regret I walked around with every day, believing that I needed to be judged and punished. I also forgave myself for abusing the little girl who did not know any better because no one had taught her better.

Little Helenne had been stuck in my grown up body for decades and by forgiving myself, I liberated her. I look at my younger self differently now. Little Helenne is still a part of me and I'm a part of her. Except now, she's different. Little Helenne is different because I'm different. She's different because she's me. And I am her. My childhood self is no longer broken but to this day, little Helenne and I continue to work on ourselves. We have learned much along the way and we continue to learn more. Little Helenne has helped me tremendously throughout my spiritual journey. And I have done the same for her. I used to think she was a frail little thing, but I've come to see that little Helenne is a survivor. She has fought to be where she is today. But she doesn't have to fight anymore. She doesn't have to be a survivor either. Little Helenne doesn't have to be anything but be. She can live freely now, knowing God is the parent she currently has, always has had, and will forever have. I look out for her and she for me. We coexist beautifully. We are one. We are the same. We were always meant to be.

As I am writing this my heart is overflowing with love and acceptance for myself as well as for you, my brother or sister, who is currently reading my story. I believe we are connected and through our connection I pray that when we are faced with difficult situations, we remember to love and accept ourselves in the same way that our Father in Heaven, the Source of All, God, accepts us. May we remember to ask our Father for help when we approach the wall of judgment and are unable to accept ourselves right away. May we remember that all we need to do is be willing to accept our Father's will for us—unconditional love. We don't have to worry about doing it all of the time or doing it perfectly. We can take comfort in knowing we just have to be willing and our Father will help us with the rest. The truth is there never was anything to forgive. It was all a learning experience. A very painful one. But then again, our most painful experiences are the ones that teach us the most.

Let us remember that forgiveness is reserved for self. It is a gift that comes from us to us, the tool that helps us break through the wall of judgment and walk towards the path to acceptance. And when we finally get to our destination, when we finally reach acceptance, we experience a sense of peace as we have never felt before. This is the serenity we had been searching for all of our lives. It's the oasis we have needed to quench our thirst. We had a taste of it throughout our journey, a little here, a little there. But this peaceful feeling had never lasted, as we relied on the things that were outside of us to make us feel whole and complete. It came in small portions, making us feel a little better, and when that feeling ran out, we felt worse than before. The peace we feel when we accept ourselves is entirely different. It comes directly from our Father in Heaven, the Source of All, God. As soon as we experience this peace, we know what it means to be free. We are finally at peace.

Peace is an inside job. It is the gift we receive from our Father at the exact moment we accept ourselves without any conditions. Peace is what we receive when we plug into our Father's unconditional love. Peace is the gift of freedom: freedom from judgment, freedom from fear, freedom from illusion. When are free, we know what it means to be. We are, not because we do a thing or don't do it, not because we love something or hate it. We are the children of God. We are, simply because we are. We are existing. We are living. We are being. That's what acceptance does for us. It teaches us to give up the fight. It frees us from judgment. It leads us to peace. It allows us to be. Just be.

PART TWO

THE TEACHINGS
OF TOMAS

"We were created in love, power, and energy. We were created to be."

CHAPTER 6

THE ART OF BEING

The Little Girl and the Old Man

ALONGSIDE OF A water well sat a little girl. She was sitting on the dirt floor, arms crossed, head lying heavily on the bricks of the well, her eyes filled with tears. The little girl had been sitting there for nearly half a day, hoping someone would talk to her, wishing someone would say something to ease her pain. Many people had come to the well. They saw the little girl crying but they paid no mind to her. They were here to fetch water, not to console a crying child. And so, after they retrieved the water for which they came, the people headed back to their village without voicing one word to the little girl. You see, the little girl wasn't a stranger to any of these people. They knew her well. She knew them as well, for she had been born and raised in their village.

Up until this morning, before she was cast away, she had been a beloved member of the village's most respected tribe.

As the midday sun rose high into the sky, the little girl started to feel more and more helpless. She could not stop herself from crying and her body was aching. She had never before experienced such a difficult day. She had prayed numerous times for peace of mind but peace had yet to come. The little girl did not know what to do, where to go, or who to be. The day was long and tiring. More and more familiar faces came to the water well and still, no one had addressed her. They stared at her for only a second and when their eyes landed on hers, the people quickly turned their heads in the other direction. The little girl might as well have been invisible. She sat there for hours and hours with her pain and loneliness as hundreds of eyes glanced at her and pretended she did not exist. Like all the people who had come to the well, time passed by without paying any attention to her. The little girl had needed someone to talk to. She had needed some words of wisdom. She had needed more time. Everything she had needed had appeared in front of her. But the door to gain entrance to her needs had been tightly shut.

The sun was starting to go down, signaling the coming of the night. For the hundredth time, the little girl reached out her hand to lift her dress so that she could wipe her teary eyes. That's when she saw the shaking in her hand. She paused to gather her strength but could find none. Her body was frail. Her mind anxious. Her spirit somnolent. It was a miracle she was still alive. The little girl sighed, letting her hand fall to the ground. She had not eaten anything since she left the village many, many hours ago. The little girl felt so weak. She could hear the loud rumbling in her stomach, her insides twisting in deep hunger. The little girl had hoped to be strong. She had hoped to one day return home as a woman grown. She had hoped to come back to the village as a worthy member of the most respected tribe. But now, she feared her hopes had vanished into oblivion the same way her strength had. The little girl felt as though she was the biggest failure in the history of mankind. She wondered if her family had been right to send her away. She did not know who she wanted to be; therefore, she wasn't worthy of being part of anything. That's what they had told her and she was now starting to believe it.

The negative thoughts ran across her mind like wild animals. A great deal of sadness and hopelessness weighed heavily upon her already-burdened shoulders. It hit her in that instant that she had ended up down here by the water well, alone and vulnerable. Night was soon to come and here she was, a frail thing, with no one to speak to, no village to go to, and no tribe in which to belong. The little girl wondered if she would ever see her parents again. She wondered if she would feel their loving embrace. She wondered if their warm kisses would welcome her back to the place she once called home. She had been told not ever to return unless she had figured out who she wanted to be. But that hadn't yet happened. The little girl took a breath and sighed. She had been removed from what she knew, what she was comfortable with, what she loved. Life as she knew it was over. And it all happened because she had been busy being a child.

The little girl wondered if her parents were thinking of her as much as she was thinking of them. She wondered if they felt her absence, if they had looked on as she walked away, if they felt as empty as she did now that she wasn't a part of their lives anymore. The thoughts were coming faster than she could handle. It made her head ache. The little girl could feel the last of her strength evaporating from her body. She feared she would die here. Dying was the last thing she wanted. But dying alone was the last thing she needed. Though she had not yet figured out who she wanted to be, the little girl did not think she deserved to die this night. Had she not been good enough? Had she not been worthy enough? Had she not been holy enough? The thoughts made more tears well up in her eyes. They ran past her cheeks, making their way all the way down to her trembling chest. Her entire body was shivering. She had never before felt so alone. She was getting weaker and weaker. No matter how much she hated to think of it, the little girl knew sooner or later death would come. Of that, she had no doubt.

Something cracked in the distance!!! The loud,

creepy sound sent her heart pounding in a frenzy. *Boom-boom! Boom-boom! Boom-boom!* The little girl quickly lifted her head toward the sky, her eyes wide open, staring into the distance. Her heart was beating so fast. *Boom-boom! Boom-boom! Boom-boom!* Quickly, she wrapped her arms around her tiny body, shutting her eyes as tightly as she could. *Boom-boom! Boom-boom! Boom-boom!* Something was coming. She could feel it. *Boom-boom! Boom-boom! Boom-boom!* Her jaw trembled. Her life flashed before her eyes. Her lungs puffed in and out of control as her heart went *Boom! Boom! Boom!* Death had come for her. *Boom!* Death was approaching closer. *Boom!* Death was here. *Boom!*

"Who are you?" a voice asked.

"Please don't take me," replied the little girl, with a faint whisper. "I'm not ready to die."

"When will you be ready?" the voice asked, assertively.

"I don't know," answered the little girl. "I'm not ready to die."

"No one has ever been ready for death," the voice said, laughing.

The little girl opened her eyes. To her surprise, there was a man sitting beside her—a very old man.

"Who are you?" she asked him.

"Nighttime comes," the old man said. "Best to find your way home."

"I have no home."

"Everyone has a home."

"Not me," said the little girl, lowering her eyes. "Not anymore."

"What happened?"

"It's a long story."

"Lucky for you," the old man said, shaking his head and smiling, "I have nothing but time."

And so she told him her story. The little girl was twelve years old, just a few days shy of thirteen, the age of becoming a woman. But before she could be a woman, she had to decide who she wanted to be for the rest of her life. It was the way of her people, a very old tradition of the tribe. Problem was, the little girl did not know who to be. As the day of womanhood approached, she became more and more confused, not knowing who to be. She had brought shame upon her family and was not allowed to return to the village until she figured out who she wanted to be. Her people believed it was the only way to remove the shame and restore honor unto the family, as were their customs. That's why she had been sent away. She had wanted to fulfill their wishes, she truly had. Earlier this morning, she had the strongest conviction that one day she would have figured it out, but now she wasn't so sure.

"I was hoping someone would help me choose who I wanted to be," the little girl said to the old man when she finished telling him her story. "But no one who came to the well wanted to speak to me."

The old man stared at her, his head bouncing up and down and up and down. "No one can help you choose who you want to be," he told her. "In fact, you can't even choose who you want to be."

"I can't?" the little girl asked, her eyes widening in curiosity.

"There is no such thing. You already are."

"But I don't know who I am," said the little girl.

"Even when don't know who you are, you are."

"But what am I to do for the rest of my life?"

"What you do is what you do. Who you are is who you are."

"What do you mean?" the little girl asked, not fully grasping what the old man had said.

"What you do can change. Who you are can never change."

The little girl paused. "I never thought of it that way."

The old man smiled. He then got up and started to walk away.

"Where are you going?" the little girl asked.

"Nowhere," the old man replied, as he continued his walk. "I'm just being."

The little watched the old man go about his way, but something within her had invigorated. She didn't know how it was possible but she felt stronger than she ever had. She pulled herself from the floor and ran after the old man. She followed him for nearly an hour without either of them saying a word to each other. She knew the old man had seen her but he hadn't yet acknowledged her presence. She did not care. For hours into the night, the little girl continued to follow the old man. After a while, the old man paused. He turned and looked at her.

"What is the reason you have been following me?" the old man asked her.

"I'm not following you," answered the little girl. "I'm just being."

The old man smiled. He knew that the little girl as young as she was had understood the meaning of the art of being. And so, he became her mentor. Not to teach her things she did not already know. But to help her remove the blocks life would lay on her path that would stop her from being the person she had been created to be, from being who she already was.

The Precious and Priceless Gift of Being

There were so many times in my life when I wanted to be something other than who I already was. I wanted to lose weight so that I could become thin so that I could be happy. I wanted to stop shopping so that I could get myself out of debt so that I could save money so that I could be able to properly provide for myself. In my heart, I knew that I did not really want to stop shopping because shopping made me happy. And the more I tried to get myself to stop shopping, the faster I ran to the mall every chance I got. Have you ever tried to focus on getting rid of something in your life and the more you focus on it, the bigger the space it takes up in your life. That was my ongoing struggle with shopping.

I could not be with it nor could I be without it. We had a need-based relationship, where two parts of myself were constantly fighting each other. A part of me fought really hard to stop me from shopping. The other part fought just as hard to keep me shopping.

Another thing I wanted was to have a great deal of money. One of my heart's desires was to buy a condo on the beach. In my mind, which I must say was insane at the time, I thought I needed the condo so that I would have easy access to the beach at all hours of the day and all hours of the night. I thought that living so near to the beach meant that I could get rid of my anxiety once and for all. And with no anxious thoughts to disturb my mind, I could finally be at peace. Boy, did I crave to be at peace!

Believe it or not, I got pretty much everything I wanted, and none of it gave me the happiness nor the peace I was seeking. I lost weight. I became very thin. I even stopped shopping for a while, but not long enough to save the money I needed for the down payment on my desired beach condo. The truth is, from where I was living, I could have gone to the beach every day if that was what I really wanted to do. I love the beach, I really do. But somewhere along my journey, God must have injected some sanity in my crazy mind, making me vividly aware that even if I lived as near as possible to the beach, even if I indeed spent twenty four hours of each and every day at the beach, none of it would have brought me peace. In fact, spending so much time there would have probably made me more insane than I already was.

As Tomas often says, "Peace is an inside job." It isn't something that can be fulfilled on the outside of ourselves. It must be fulfilled within. Looking for peace, joy, love, empowerment, completion, and wholeness outside of ourselves is a waste of our precious time. Even if we manage to get these things from the outside, it doesn't work. We feel safe and secure for a moment but the second our sense of security vanishes, we're left off worse than where we were before. Everything that makes up who and what we are resides deep inside of us. With that said, there is absolutely no need to become anything at all. We already are.

We are wherever we go. We are however we do. We are with whomever we meet. We *are*, no matter what circumstance crosses our paths. We are because we are. We have always been and we will always be. This is the truth of our natural essence. We were created in love, power, and energy. We were created to be. There is no greater gift, no greater blessing than to be. To be is to believe in who we are. To be is to live our lives in a way that honors our natural essence. We can choose not to demonstrate this truth. We can choose to walk away from it. We can even choose to make several attempts at destroying it. But the fact of the matter is, deep inside of all of us, we have never and will never stop being who we are.

As children we were often asked who and what we wanted to be when we grew into adulthood. We were taught to go to school. And this was the beginning of many beginnings. We were told to earn good grades so that we could graduate so that we could get into the best colleges. But getting into college wasn't enough. We needed to study hard, very hard, so that we could get a degree so that we could have respectable jobs so that we could earn money. We were told over and over again that we needed money so that we could provide a decent lifestyle for ourselves and our families. But it didn't end here. We also needed to save for retirement as well as leave enough money behind for those we loved. Throughout most of our life, we were told over and over to strive for better and better and to compete for more and more. But somewhere along the way, some of us realized we would never catch up, as there was always something else to seek. We started to question if there would ever be an end to the constant chasing, the competition, the need to find the next thing. Yet, we couldn't just jump out of the race. How would we then survive in this word that demands we become more and more? We needed to hold on for the next thing, and the next thing, and the next thing. Out in the world we went, day after day, seeking to be more and more and more than what we already werc.

Now, this isn't to say that we are not to pursue a better education or apply for a better-paying job. Life is about improvement, both inside and outside. However, we must take care of our insides first. As previously stated, everything that makes up who we are resides inside of us. Feel free to want a better car, house, and career. Feel free to chase your dreams. Feel free to believe that you can have everything your heart desires and that God will give it to you. God wants nothing but the very best for us, His children. God's desire is to elevate us beyond our wildest imagination. But we are not to seek anything that resides outside of ourselves with the intention of becoming more or less than who we already are. I didn't need to lose weight and become thin to be happy. Happiness lives within me. I didn't need to have a condo at the beach in order to be at peace. Peace resides within me. I am happiness. I am peace. I am because I am. You are because you are. We are because we are. This is the way God created us to be. This is what makes us such remarkable creatures—the art of being.

What a gift it is to be. We don't have to be anything extra or less than because everything we need to be and everything we want to be, we already are. We are the amazing work of art of the Most High God. The art of being is being in the flow of life. The art of being is living life in a way that reflects our authentic selves inside and out. The art of being is the recognition that everything we are, everything we want, everything we need, resides within us. The art of being is the awareness that the key that opens the golden door of our lives dwells deep within us. The art of being is the demonstration to ourselves, God, and our brothers and sisters that we know and believe in who we are. To be a work of God is to be the most precious and priceless work of art. To be God's work of art is a privilege—the greatest honor. We are marvelous. We are godlike. Thank you, God, for creating us. Thank you for the precious and priceless gift of being.

*"When you can't love you, God
will love you. And when you can
love you, God will still love you.
God's love is forever constant."*

CHAPTER 7

THROUGHOUT ETERNITY

FROM THE MOMENT we arrived on this Earth, we have been schooled on who we are, the environment in which we live, and on the best ways to navigate through this thing called life. As we grew into adulthood, we learned to make our own decisions about what we wanted or did not want, who we were or weren't, and what we believed to be true or false. We lived life the best way in which we had learned to live it, both through other people as well as through our own experiences. When we came to have children of our own, we passed onto them the knowledge we had acquired throughout our journey of life. The following years of our lives flew by. Time went faster and faster and before we noticed, we had grown old.

Anyone can die at any given moment, under any given circumstance. Death does not discriminate.

However, there is something about reaching the golden years of life that makes one clearly realize that death is not too far away. This isn't necessarily a bad thing. Hopefully throughout the years, there came a point in our lives when we found out who we were and our purpose here on Earth. Some of us were fortunate enough to look back and reflect and ask some questions about the meaning of it all. If our consciousness had grown to a higher level of awareness, where it was willing to open up to the unlimited possibilities of our existence, we came to believe that death was just the shedding of our outer shell and that it is a natural step in the process of life. This step, while not our favorite topic of conversation, is crucial in returning us to the pure, natural state in which we had been created—energy, love, and power. Death comes to us all. Not because we are unworthy. Not because we have done something wrong. Not because we have been bad. Death is a biological and spiritual part of life. Some die in infancy or childhood, while others die much later. Sooner or later, we all must leave our bodies. We do so because we are all so much more than our bodies. This isn't the end. It's the beginning.

Upon Mother Earth, death is described as the end of life. But in the world of Spirit, being born in the body is actually what is considered death, for when the soul descends upon this material world, it passes through the veil of oblivion. As a result, the soul forgets itself. It must then travel through a human and spiritual journey in order to remember everything it has forgotten but already knew. Contrary to what we have been taught, death in the body is truly the act of being born. It's the return of the soul to its knowing center. The return to our pure natural essence. We don't really die. We just go home.

Some people are uncomfortable with the idea of reincarnation because it does not fit into what they have previously been taught or currently believe to be true. Other people, however, are uncomfortable with the term because they fear turning into an ant, a bird, a plant, a tree, or anything that is outside of their control. Let me assure you of the fact that if you choose to incarnate upon Mother Earth—and I say choose because incarnation is a choice—you, as a human being, will never come back as a cat or a dog or anything other than a human being. We all get to choose whether or not we will come back into the body. Reincarnation isn't a process forced upon us by the universe. Before we incarnate, we have complete power over the lessons we wish to learn. We choose where we are born, our race, our gender, our religion, as well as the human beings through which we will come through—our parents.

Incarnation is the process of a soul being born into a body. Reincarnation, however, is the process of a soul being born into a body for the second, or third, or hundredth time. There are no limits upon how many times a soul can reincarnate. We can reincarnate infinitely if this is what we desire to do. Every living and breathing creation on this planet is a soul that has incarnated itself into physical form.

There are trillions and trillions of souls throughout all of God's universes. And each soul created by God is made of a unique natural essence at the moment of conception. A soul's natural essence will always incarnate into its own physical form of energy. This means a soul's natural essence will always remain true to itself. In other words, a soul created at the consciousness level of incarnating itself into a human body isn't able to come back as a cat or a dog. Nor can a soul that was created at the consciousness level of incarnating itself into a cat or a dog manifest into the human form. The universe is a perfectly ordered system. Beings aren't just randomly coming into existence out of the blue. If God wants more souls to manifest themselves upon Mother Earth as cats or dogs, He would surely create them as He certainly has the power to do so. Nothing in the universe bypasses God's perfect wisdom. What benefit would it be to God to have a soul at the consciousness level of a human incarnate into a cat or a dog? We simply wouldn't be great at it, as this was not the nature in which we were created.

Many of us have lived through several lifetimes. We have lived these lives in several different universes during several different periods of time. Many of us have been upon Mother Earth before. We have also been together with each other throughout the many past lives in which we lived. Past lives are accessed in only one way—cellular memory. Tomas often says, within every living being, there is an infinite number of cells, and each cell holds all the information of a being's life history from the first time the being incarnated upon a universe up until the very present. These cellular records are part of our soul programming. They direct us to the experiences we need by attracting the necessary teacher to bring in the lessons we have chosen to work through in our current lifetime. The only way to access our cellular memory is by passing the conscious mind and going straight through the heart. Remember, the conscious mind is the egocentric part of ourselves. This part consistently separates itself from God. However, the heart is our knowing center. It's the part of us that is directly connected to God. This is the reason why those who want to see a previous lifetime are usually put into either in a hypnotic or a deep meditative state.

Those who want to go back to see a past life usually do so through regression techniques. A regression is the process of a being going back, temporarily, to a previous lifetime. These methods have become very prominent in the last few years. Some people such as Dr. Brian Weiss believe in the process's therapeutic values, while others think its total foolishness. Whether or not to be regressed depends strictly on the individual, as it is their life and past lives. The choice is theirs. I, myself, have been regressed a few times. I strongly believe it works. Belief is a very strong motivator. Whatever one believes ultimately becomes true for them. If you believe it works, it will. If you believe it doesn't work, it won't. There is no right. There is no wrong.

We are eternal. This means that we, as the creations of God, will never go away. We will never die. We will never stop existing. We will never stop being. God is what was before the beginning. God is the beginning. He is the past. He is the now. He is the future. He is eternity and beyond. God, in His boundless, limitless, unconditional love, created us in His image and likeness. We are one with God, and in this oneness we have been made to co-exist with our Father from the very moment we were created throughout now, eternity and beyond. Wherever we are, God is. Whenever we are, God is. We can take up different forms depending on where we are at our right now moment. Nevertheless, a soul remains a soul whether or not it has a body. A soul remains a soul whether it has been through one lifetime, a dozen, a hundred, or even a thousand. We were before we were born into a body and we continue to be once we leave the body. In essence of who we are, the word "reincarnation" is almost unnecessary because our natural essence had never changed no matter what our outer layer reflected.

Many clients who come to see Tomas have asked about reincarnation and how much bearing it has for them in this lifetime. Since all of life is about lessons, we choose which ones we will experience. How important is it for you to understand when and where the lessons actually occurred? If you came in this lifetime with a fear of water and drowning, and you have discovered that this fear originated from a past life where you actually did drown, how does knowing this information serve you in the present? The need to understand comes from the intellectual mind, the ego, and not from the heart, which is our knowing. The heart is our power plug to our God-consciousness. The heart just knows what is true and what is not. Unlike the intellectual mind, it needs no proof. The heart doesn't ask why, or when, or how. This isn't to say that one must not seek to understand but rather to make one aware that whether or not he or she understands where and when the fear originated, he or she will still have to do the work required to walk through the fear. There is no shortcut to healing. We must always do the work.

I have been able to see two of my own past lifetimes here on Earth. I know there have been many more, but so far I've only seen two. The first life I was able to see on my own a number of times in between the moments of waking up from sleep and becoming fully alert. This was before reincarnation and regression therapy were recognized and popularized. In that life, I was a high priestess in ancient Egypt, a mistress of the Pharaoh. I looked very different then: small and petite, with dark hair. I governed a temple that believed in the One Supreme

God, also called the One Supreme Being. Other deities had their own temples, and I used to worship them as well, but I came to only believe in the One Supreme Being. I was warned countless times to change my beliefs but I refused to do so. I knew in my heart that there weren't several gods. One God was all there was, and I remained loyal to what I knew to be true in my heart. As a result, I was thrown into a snake pit, where I died.

In my current lifetime, I have always felt a strong dislike of snakes. I never understood where this came from, as I could not recall having a terrible experience that I knew of in this lifetime. I now know that my distaste of snakes originated from a previous lifetime. Till this day, I cannot bear to think about or see them, not even in pictures. The mere thought of snakes makes my blood boil. Though I know where my fear originated, I have no desire to cure myself of this phobia, as I have no plans to befriend a snake. I avoid the places they frequent and when I pray, I ask God to please keep them from my home. The snakes can have their world. I have mine.

The second lifetime was in Roanoke, West Virginia, where I was a Southern Belle. The first time I visited that life, I was watching myself from the back. I was eighteen years old, the oldest of three children. I had a younger brother and another small sister. I had dark hair and was again small and petite. I was wearing a pink ruffled dress. The material was like taffeta, with small little ruffles and small puffed up sleeves. I saw myself standing on the porch of a large white house with large white pillars. Someone was coming up the steps to see me. It was a man. He was wearing a grey jacket and pants. He had a long knife hanging from his waist, falling down the side of his leg. This man was coming to tell me goodbye and that he would see me when he returned. I knew he was in love with me. And I knew that he would get killed and that I would never see him again. In that lifetime, knowing this didn't bother me one bit.

I have met this man in my current life. The very first time I saw him, I felt that I knew him and in that very instant, I fell in love. It was quite an experience. I later found out through regression where we had met before. He looked different in this current life than he did in the past, but I had no doubt that he was the soldier who had come to say goodbye to me. In the past lifetime, he had loved me profoundly and I kept rejecting him. In this lifetime, I loved him deeply and he kept rejecting me.

Karma is about experiencing unlearned lessons. One way or another, we always get the opportunity to experience the other side of the choices we make. This isn't a punishment and it isn't to be looked upon in judgment. This is just one of the spiritual laws of the universe. What you give, you will receive. Sometimes it's in the same lifetime; other times, the lessons cycle forward to a future lifetime. It took a while, but eventually, I did release the love I had for this man. Today, I almost never think of him at all. Our history is finished and laid to rest. Years later, I ran into him again. I had no reaction to seeing him, other than surprise. I knew in my heart that we were over. The karmic debt had been paid. Balance had been restored.

I have been asked many times if animals reincarnate as we do. The answer is yes, they do. Our animal friends are very close to us. They are part of our Spirit family. A lot of times, they have been with us before. In this universe, humans reincarnate as humans and never as anything else. We do, however, change gender and race. Similarly, animals do not change their species. But they can change their type. A dog will never come back as a cat, but a domestic cat can return as anything in the cat family, such as a lion or a tiger or any member of the feline family. It is the same with birds. Birds return as birds.

My Quaker parrot Bugie, who is still with me today, has been with me in two previous incarnations: once as an eagle and once as a hawk. Bugie is my protector. He likes to watch over me by sitting above my head when I'm lying down. This is the same thing he had done before, only now he has a smaller body. Our animal friends are similar to us in that they also get to choose their lessons. They are also blessed with angelic helpers, as we are. Similar to the human bond of love, the animal bond of love is not broken after they make their transition to the Spirit world. They have the same ability as their human counterparts to come and visit with their loved ones and assist them in times of need.

Animals have the gift of free will, as we do. They can choose to return and come back into another body. Sometimes, it's because they have unfinished lessons, or just that their soul desires to come back. Animals are teachers of unconditional love. It breaks my heart to see them abused. I used to get very angry towards those who abuse animals. I couldn't understand how some people could be so cruel. Tomas has explained to me that people who abuse animals are incapable of accepting unconditional love. They hate themselves so badly that they project their inner-hate onto the animal, for what's inside must always come out. It's a blessing to have an animal be a part of our lives. They love us no matter what. Unconditional love is the greatest gift we can ever receive from God, human, or animal.

Death in the body, as we know it upon Mother Earth, exists because our Spirit is boundless while our human bodies are not. Our natural state of being is limitless; inhabiting a body is not. Living in the body situation has many limits. For a boundless soul, coming into the body is a very shocking experience. This is why a female entity will be pregnant for a period of time. A baby doesn't just appear out of thin air. When a soul chooses to return, the soul is assigned a Most High guide, a Guardian Angel, as well as the other members of their Spirit family. These Spirit Helpers, as they are called, are here to assist the soul throughout their journey of life.

There is a golden cord of energy that connects the soul to the Spirit world while the soul is being covered with a physical body into its mother's womb. By the time a baby enters the physical world, the soul has, for the most part, acclimated to the limitations of the body. When we make the transition known as death, the golden thread that holds our soul within our body is released. Our soul essence is then free and able to return to the world in which it was created. The world of oneness and wholeness. The world where only love exists.

When we return to our natural essence, it is a bit of a shock. To help us adjust to our new situation, we have what we call a charger that we sit upon in order to acclimate to the change of coming from a limited physical world to a limitless spirit world. Sitting upon this charger is how we regain balance. Our essence is recharged, similar to a cordless appliance that has used up all of its energy. During that time, we are able to review all of our past incarnations as well as what we have learned and what we have not. This is not a time of judgment. There no judgment in Spirit. Remember, in God's world, there is only oneness and love. People who pass on naturally will need less time to recharge than those who have experienced a traumatic death such as a car accident, homicide, or suicide. When a traumatic sequence occurs, the essence of the being will require more time on the charger than someone who has made a peaceful transition. We have the ability to reincarnate immediately after the regeneration process if we choose to do so. We may also choose to spend more time in the Spirit world. The choice is always ours to make.

Sometimes, when we reincarnate, we have not completely released all aspects of the previous incarnation. This is the reason a person can feel attracted to the same sex and/or feel as though they are trapped in the wrong body. When the previous ties of a past incarnation have not been completely severed, the being will bring the remembrances with them when they come into the new body. As stated before, a soul has the power to choose when to return. Sometimes it's too early. They return before they have released the sexual and/or gender aspects of the previous incarnation; therefore, it's still a part of them. This isn't good. It isn't bad. It just is.

I have been asked many times if suicide has any karmic effect on the person coming back into another incarnation. Suicide occurs when a being makes the conscious choice to no longer remain in the body. They end their own lives way before their time is up. First, I must say that suicide is an option available to everyone, as is the choice to live. There is no punishment for those who choose to go home earlier than the time they had previously agreed to. We have a God of unconditional love. He welcomes us home no matter our choices. However, make no mistake. There are many lessons to be incurred for those who chose to end their lives. These lessons are not coming from punishment. They come from love. Lessons are nothing to be frightened of. They are here to help the being grow and learn. Sometimes, a being isn't ready to accept the lessons they have signed up for in a particular lifetime. And so they leave and wait to work through these lessons when they reincarnate again at another time. When a being makes an early transition, all unlearned lessons will be brought forward to the next lifetime, in addition to the new lessons that the being chooses to learn. This is the exact reason why the next lifetime after suicide is usually extremely difficult. In the case of taking one's own life, the being will receive lessons to teach them about what they have left behind for their loved ones. The saying "You will reap what you sow" is true. A being who has committed suicide will have to work through the lessons of guilt and regret when they incarnate again. Throughout his or her entire life, or perhaps several other lives, the being will receive what they have previously given to others until balance is restored.

Throughout most of my life, I have often entertained thoughts of suicide. But I have never acted on them. However, I did come very close once. I had reached a point where extreme weariness in my mind, body, and soul was the only feeling I could feel. There were many dark days and many dark nights when I could see no light. There were times when I was so weary, I could barely roll myself over on the bed, let alone get out of the bed. I used to feel the beatings pounding against my chest, but instead of thinking it was my heart, I thought it was a foreign object beating inside of me, pumping pain and misery throughout my veins. I have never known so much pain. I didn't know how to make any of it go away. Deep down inside, I don't think I really wanted to die. But I felt that dying was the way to end the pain.

One of the spiritual laws of manifestation is that you will create what you focus upon. The more you focus on a thought, the faster the thought will manifest into reality. I was a master at creating major fears for myself more than once throughout my life. But the latest fear that I had been left to deal with was the one that almost sent me over the edge. For many years, I had this great fear that I would one day become physically ill, alone, and without any money to take care of my basic needs. I was obsessed with thinking about it. I constantly worried about becoming sick, extremely worried about being alone, and was sick-to-my-stomach worried that I would have no money to provide for myself. I used to pray to God over and over to please not let this nightmare become a reality in my life. I spent hours, days, weeks, begging and bargaining with God to please not let me get sick. I prayed and prayed until one day everything I had worried about, everything I had obsessed over, and everything I had feared was staring at me right in my face.

I was ill with a herniated disc, in tremendous pain, alone, with barely any money to my name.

I had gotten hurt at work, and all of my friends walked away from me. My friends could not deal with my negativity. I don't blame them. I, myself, could not deal with my negativity. Unlike a bad dream, there was no waking up from this nightmare that had become my reality. It was the most painful thing I've had to deal with. Wherever I turned, I saw no hope. However I turned, I saw no hope. The last straw was when the newspaper called me because I didn't pay the bill. When I told them that workmen's comp had not paid me for three months, they told me not to worry, I would still have the newspaper. But the minute I got off the phone with them, I hit rock bottom. The pain, the fear, the extreme hopelessness all became too much to bear. I decided that I had enough—Tomas or no Tomas, God or no God, I did not want to be here any longer. I was going to put an end to my misery. And I was going to do so by killing myself.

My bird Bugie was the vehicle God used to save me from myself. This is one of the many important reasons why I love my bird wholeheartedly. He has always been my protector, even when the protection is from myself. It was about two o'clock in the morning when I was about to go through with it. I was sitting on the edge of my bed, writing the suicide note, believing there was no use of me being here. I couldn't see any part of my life that was working. For a very long time, I had often felt I had never belonged on this Earth, but now I believed I no longer needed to be on this Earth. I felt as though I was a huge, dark ball of extreme pain. Not only was I in pain, I was the pain. There was no escaping the pain that was myself.

I was holding a bottle of pills in my hand, about to put an end to it all when suddenly I wondered what would happen to my bird. My heart stopped. In the suicide note I was writing, I thought about asking a very good friend to take care of Bugie. Suddenly, I remembered my friend was in a relationship and her partner hated birds. Not a second passed by before I heard a loud and resounding "NO" in my head. I knew it was my friend's partner and that she would not let my friend accept Bugie. My beautiful bird had been there for me so many times. He was my first physical introduction to learning how to love. I couldn't bear the thought of leaving him all alone. And in that moment, I chose to live. Not for myself, not for Tomas, not the channeling, not even for God. I chose to live for my beautiful bird whom I loved so very much.

Two weeks after my suicide attempt, I visited my friend at her house. Her partner was there. I had never before told any of them what had happened that night. But as I walked in the house I saw my friend's partner, the one who did not like birds, lying in bed. She was home from work because of a migraine. That's when she began to tell me the story. "Two weeks ago, I had a dream about you," she said, in a voice that sent a vicious chill through my bones. "I dreamt you were going to kill yourself and you were going to give us Bugie.

I sat up in bed and yelled out NO!" I looked at her and paused. There was nothing I could say. Then I laughed and without thinking about it, the words tumbled out of my mouth. "I heard you, and that's the only reason why I didn't do it." She looked at me with wide eyes.

Overcoming my suicide attempt was extremely difficult. But once it was over, I grew into a stronger person. Ever since that night, I have never thought about suicide again. I have had days when the feeling of utter hopelessness comes over me and have had times when it crossed my mind to leave my body, but not through suicide. God will take me home when it's my time to go. I know better now. I have been able to share my experiences with others who want to leave this world, feeling that there's no other way to end the pain. At the time when I was going to kill myself, I had no inkling of the wreckage suicide leaves behind for those left behind on this Earth. I strongly believe God touched me that night and stopped me, but I know ultimately the choice was mine to make. I'm so grateful I chose to stay. I belong here on this Earth because wherever I am, God is. And I belong with God. The life I currently have is one filled with abundant gifts, opportunities, blessings, love, joy, and peace. I cannot express enough how grateful I am to God for rescuing me from making such an unloving mistake.

After that incident, I started to attract clients that were either suicidal or had lost a loved one to suicide. Some of them would walk into my house and within seconds, I would immediately recognize the level of pain and suffering they were trapped in. These people were stuck in tremendous grief, suffering, and guilt about their role in their loved one's suicide. Those who are left behind are usually tortured by an immeasurable amount of regret. They have the belief that there was something they could have done and did not do in order to prevent their loved one from killing themselves. This of course, isn't true. However, in the moment, it's the illusion that appears real to them and they cling to it like there's no tomorrow.

When someone is truly determined to do something, whatever the thing may be, the only people that can stop them are themselves. God, Himself, in all of His power, all of His wisdom, and all of His love, cannot stop a soul from taking his or her life if the soul will not allow it. God, the Father in Heaven, the Source of All, has given to each of his creations many, many gifts. But there is a most sacred one. This sacred gift is called free will. Choice is the right for each of us to choose. It is our heritage and birthright. Not even the Father in Heaven can touch free will. It is the most sacred blessing we receive from God, and it must be honored by all. Sometimes the choices we make are very loving. Other times, they are the direct opposite. It is very karmic to infringe upon the free will of another. We don't have to like the choices our loved ones make. But we must honor their right to choose.

Suicide occurs when a being loses all hope and cannot see the light that is shining at end of the tunnel. They believe they are a burden to those they love and that their loved ones as well as the entire world will be better off without them. During this dark period in their lives, the beings who are contemplating suicide are only able to look at one side of the coin and not the other. I don't believe anyone would commit suicide if they realized the pain and suffering they would leave behind for those they loved. Perhaps some would go through with it. Perhaps not. Only God truly knows. Guilt, regret, anger, frustration, pain, and misery is the foundation of the legacy one leaves behind for their loved ones after taking their own life. This legacy remains long after the being has gone home. And it takes a great deal of effort to move beyond it.

Our eternity as well as all the other gifts we receive from God is our heritage and birthright. These gifts can never be taken from us. They are ours to do with as we please. However, we must remember that life is a precious gift given to us by our Creator, the Source of all, God, and we have to do the best we can to honor this gift.

To end one's life is to spit in the image of God. It is to say that God made a mistake, that God did too little or too much, that God is wrong, that God's perfect work of art isn't perfect. None of this is true. We are better than this. We owe it to ourselves and to our Creator to honor the lifetime we have will-ingly signed up for. Life isn't a journey filled with only roses and honey. Sometimes it gets tough—really, really tough. This is the very reason we have

God, our guides, our angels, and our entire spiritual family. We aren't left to travel through this journey all alone without any guidance or support. God is with us today, tomorrow, throughout eternity and beyond. Our Father in Heaven loves us so very much. Learning to love ourselves is the least we can do to honor His everlasting, unconditional love.

No matter how dark the hour, no matter how painful the day, no matter how big the void in our hearts, God is with us. He has never and will never abandon us. God can fill what we cannot, heal what we cannot, illuminate what we cannot. We aren't alone. God is with us during every second, every minute, every hour of each and every day. He loves us immensely. He loves us infinitely. We can trust and believe in God's love. Tomas says when you can't love you, God will love you. And when you can love you, God will still love you. God's love is forever constant. He knows us inside and out. God surrounds us with more love than we can ever want, more love than we can ever need. Loving us is what God does best.

"Everything is possible and beyond possibility."

CHAPTER 8

OUR SPIRITUAL FAMILY

THERE IS AN image that forms in our mind as soon as we hear the word "alien." This image can make us feel warm inside. Or it can leave us feeling cold. It depends on our perception of the word. When we hear the word "alien," some of us picture someone who isn't from our country. It's those people who have left the land on which they were born and have immigrated onto our land. Other people who hear the word don't think of another person at all. They automatically picture a being who isn't from this world. I always find it humorous that "aliens" are described as species or beings from another world because we all are from another world. If we were to abide to the human definition of an alien, we could easily conclude that we are all aliens. None of us were created here. We came from the Spirit world. We are not from this Earth. We are but mere explorers.

There are many upon Mother Earth who have the belief that family members are those who share the same bloodline. There is truth in this statement. But let's not forget that Earth is but a tiny ball of sand in comparison to the gigantic world of God. In God's eyes, our true family isn't recognized by blood but rather by a heart-to-heart connection. Our human family isn't the only family we have. We have an immense spiritual family, which consists of both human beings and other beings in spirit. When we chose to come here, God knew we needed help. And so He devised a perfect plan to provide us with everything we would ever need. Just like our human family, our Spirit family is part of God's perfect plan for us. The primary difference between the two is that our human family deals with the lessons of the duality within while our Spirit family does not. Our human family can only be physically present with us for a certain period of time, whereas our Spirit family is always with us.

Most High Guide

Before we incarnate into a body, we choose our life lessons that will help us grow in this lifetime. It is also during this time that we attract to ourselves a guide who chooses to learn similar lessons as us. This guide is referred to as our Most High Guide. While we are learning our lessons while being in the body, our Most High Guide learns the same lessons while remaining in the Spirit world. Our Most High

Guide is given to us before we incarnate in order to assist us with the lessons we are learning. They guide us toward our highest good. When we choose to listen to them, they help us move through our life lessons easily and effortlessly.

Some guides have never been in a physical body and therefore don't understand the lesson of duality. Thankfully, most of us have guides that have incarnated before and are very familiar with the body situation. Most guides stay with us throughout our entire lifetime. However, during times of great growth, a guide may leave so that another guide may come in. When this occurs, it is almost as though a piece of ourselves has died. There is a grieving period, and afterwards, we assimilate to our new guide, who also assists us toward our highest and greatest good.

Some people have wondered if their loved ones who have passed away are their guides. Tomas says that our loved ones who have physically been with us throughout an incarnation and have made the transition to Spirit are not our Most High Guide. However, they can act as a guide for us in times of need. Love is the strongest bond there is. And when that bond is formed, it cannot be broken. Nothing precedes love in strength. Even when our loved ones have departed from this world, we are still connected to them through our love for them and their love for us. Some may wonder how this can be possible. To this, Tomas answers that everything is possible and beyond possibility. Limits have no place in the limitless world of God.

We always have the option to maintain the relationship with our loved ones even though we cannot see them in human form. We have the ability to contact them anytime we choose. Our loved ones who have departed hear us clearly, and they usually come forward when they are called. They have the ability to see and hear us, as well as transcend though time and space. In times of great need, it is their great pleasure to assist us. Unlike our Most High Guide and Guardian Angels, our departed loved ones are not constantly with us. This isn't their job in the Spirit world. They have their own purpose they must fulfill. But they look in on us from time to time, making sure we are all right. When they visit us, they use our senses to make their presence known. They do this by bypassing the conscious mind and connecting directly to our hearts. Our sense of smell is one of their favorites, as well as a slight feeling of air over a shoulder.

Guardian Angel

When a soul comes into its mother's womb, it is given a Guardian Angel. Our Guardian Angel's sole purpose is to guide and protect us through unseen events. They take care of us while we are in the body. They protect us in times of danger by doing their utmost to keep us safe. Our Guardian Angels stay with us throughout our entire incarnation up until we leave the body and the golden thread is cut. Only then do they leave our side. There is no gender in Spirit. Our Angelic Helpers, who stay on the other side and help us throughout our incarnation, are neither male nor female. They will sometimes use gender so we can easily identify with them. But they do not have physical bodies. They are just pure energy.

Fairies

Fairies are also part of our Spirit family. They are the spirits of laughter and play. They sit over our shoulders, bringing lightness and laughter into our lives. Our Fairies love it when we have a good time. They have a great sense of humor. Their presence is always overflowing with laughter and joy. When we laugh, they laugh with us. When we play, they play with us.

We have a habit of taking everything so seriously. Life isn't designed to be taken seriously all of the time. There is a time for everything. A time to work, a time to reflect, a time to play. We need to play more. We need to laugh at ourselves more. Not in a critical way, but a loving way. Play is one of the most helpful tools that helps us navigate easily through our life journey. Yet it is also one of the tools we overlook the most. We often get confused and think that work is play. It is not. Work is work. Play is play. They are two very different words and belong to two very different worlds. We like to think we can incorporate both worlds together, but we cannot. The universe simply does not work this way.

When we are doing something because we are looking for a specific result, it is not play. It is work. When we are enjoying something just because we love it, without any thought of a result, it is play. Have you ever watched a child play? He or she is fully present in the moment. The child is just being. There is no result in his or her mind. Play is about just being. It is the most healing gift we can give to our bodies and our souls. It heals the Spirit and the physical being simultaneously. Our Fairies are here to assist us with creating lightness in our energy field. They help to bring out the child that resides within all of us. When we allow ourselves to play and simply be, we are allowing our body temple to regenerate and rejuvenate. It used to be difficult for me to allow myself to laugh and play. But through-out the years I've come to realize that nothing is so shattering when I have a sense of humor about it.

Spirit Helpers

We have many helpers in the Spirit world: the ones we came with and the love connections we make here on the Earth. As previously stated, when a human being makes a bond of love with another human being, that bond is never broken—not even through the transition of physical death. It always surprises me how reluctant people are to ask their Spirit Helpers for help. It is as though they don't want to bother them with their stuff. We believe we can only ask for help with important, life-changing incidents, when really we can ask for help for just about anything. Our Spirit Helpers are part of our spiritual family. They are always eager to help. They only wait for our permission, as they are unable to violate our free will.

It is a great comfort for me to know that I am not alone. I love knowing that my Spirit family is available to help me with everything I need. I feel very close to them and truly enjoy their presence in my life. If you wish to build your relationship with your Spirit Helpers, I recommend starting out slowly. Ask for small, unimportant things in order to start building a relationship based on trust and faith. Try asking for a parking place or getting to an appointment on time. It's easy. What's not always easy is to hear or see the clear signs that are being provided when you are hysterical because of your own doubt and fears. Keep at it. With practice, you will be able to hear and see the signs more clearly. When you have built a relationship with your Spirit family and something important comes along, it will be easier for you to ask for assistance. I have found that "the guys" (my nickname for my Spirit Helpers) are very funny. I ask them for everything: work, affordable restaurants, perfect presents for others and for myself. It amazes me how much they are on target. Why struggle to find the answers when all I have to do is ask?

Sometimes we look at certain situations in confusion because we are frozen in fear, stuck, unable to move forward. When this occurs, we don't have to waste our time being paralyzed. We can ask our Spirit Helpers for signs of what to do, or we can ask God directly. God's will for all of us is one thing and one thing only—love. In God's world, there is nothing but love. When I ask God for His will for me, I know I will get a loving response. I don't need to know what it will be, when it will be, or how it will be. I don't worry at all because I know that whatever it is, whenever it comes, however it comes, it will be God's loving choice for me. I love God with every cell of my body and I know, trust, and believe that He loves me the same. I am no longer afraid to ask God for His help because I know God wants the very best for me. God is there for me and always will be. At last, I know and believe.

Other Guides

After a few years with Tomas, I received another guide at the beach. Trielle was his name. He was very different than Tomas. Trielle had never inhabited a body, and his energy was very high. When he was housed in my body, I could not wear anything that was binding, such as a bra or rings. Trielle could not control the vibration of his energy, and he would expand my body. I once found myself channeling him for some friends. When I came back, I was almost naked; my bra was undone, my pants were open, my shoes and earrings had all come off. Anything that encumbered me or resisted expansion was removed. I used to channel him at an archeological museum in front of a giant five-thousand-pound crystal. Some people told me I grew to nine feet tall when he was in my body. Trielle's purpose was different from Tomas's. Trielle would give information on universal subjects such as other universes. Unlike Tomas, I could not sit down while Trielle was in my body. I could never sit or stay still. I would continuously be walking. Trielle's energy was way too high for me. Since he had never incarnated into a body before, he had no concept of lowering his energy to accommodate the human body. After channeling him, I would have to go to bed for the next few days to regenerate. When I couldn't take it anymore, I finally asked him not to come back because it was too physically painful for me.

The third and last guide that I have channeled was named Thomas. He only speaks in tongues, the language of love. Thomas is a very gentle being and does healings on the body. On a conscious level, I don't understand anything he says. I know my heart does, and that is what he speaks to. I remember the day when I met my spiritual guide Tomas and he told me over and over again that he was not "Thomas." And that he was "Tomas." I felt that he had said this to me over and over in order to prepare me for Thomas.

One day I decided to go to a friend's metaphysical store because they were doing auric photographs. I have always been curious to see the difference between my guide's energies. An auric

photographic camera has the ability to photograph
the energy field that surrounds a person, encom-
passing the head and shoulder area. Different colors
have different meanings. Pink is love, green is healing, blue is power. First, I had the gentleman take
my picture alone. Then, he took the photo of me
with Tomas in my body. Then, I brought in Trielle.
The photographer had no problem taking Tomas'
picture. But when it came to Trielle's, the camera would not work. The photographer was freak-
ing out. He could not understand what was wrong
with his camera. I couldn't stop laughing. I told him
that my guide's energy was too high, and that he
was blowing the camera out. I asked Trielle to lower
his energy so that the auric picture could be taken.
He did, and then the picture was taken successfully.
Everyone in the room, with the exception of the
photographer, burst into laughter. The photographer just stood there with his mouth hanging open
in absolute amazement, staring at me as though I
had two heads. Unfortunately, Thomas, not Tomas,
had not come until sometime after the pictures were
taken, so I do not have his picture.

I have been asked which lessons my guide
Tomas would want to learn with me. Tomas has told
me that before I incarnated into my present body,
I chose to sign a spiritual contract. And he came to
assist me in the fulfillment of that contract. I had
agreed to be a teacher of the Light, and Tomas had
agreed to help me. We are part of the same Spirit
family. Souls incarnate upon Mother Earth in Spirit

families. In other words, many of us come on this Earth together. A Spirit family consists of thousands of beings—more than we can even imagine. All of us belong to a Spirit family. It is within this family that we attract our guides and angels. Guides are beings, just like us. We come together because of a common goal of shared lessons we all choose to learn. We are, however, not tied to the same growth rate. The growth rate at which one chooses to learn their lessons is strictly up to the being themselves.

As we incarnate, we interchange and play different roles in each other's lives. Sometimes we may be close relatives, such as parents, children, or mates. We may have a very close association in one lifetime, or just a nodding acquaintance in another. As previously stated, we have the ability to switch gender and race from one incarnation to another. Upon Mother Earth, the body separates each of us from each another. But in the world of Spirit, there is no separation as we have here. In Spirit, there is only oneness of thought and action. This oneness of harmonizing to a common set of lessons is what defines a Spirit family. It's all based on what we need, when we need it, and receiving it at the exact moment in which we need it.

In all of the years that I have worked with Tomas, he has never once referred to me by my name. He always calls me "she who is channel to we." One day, when I couldn't fight my curiosity any longer, I asked him why he never used my name. Tomas explained that in the world of Spirit, names are not used. We are simply recognized by our energy vibration. We are energy and energy vibrates. Each of us has our own energy vibration that is unique to us. This is how we are recognized by Spirit, and each other. There is such a thing as soul recognition. It comes without explanation—just pure knowing. Soul recognition is a connection of the heart. It is often felt immediately upon meeting a person. Have you ever had the experience when you first meet someone and it seems like you have known them forever? This is because you recognize their energy vibration and experience an instant identification. The opposite can also happen—you can experience an instant dislike for a total stranger. I've had the experience of meeting someone and immediately disliking them at first sight, without even talking to them. It was like somewhere, deep inside of me, a voice was telling me, "No. This is not a connection for me." There have been times I have chosen not to listen to this voice. I have gone ahead only to find out how true my inner knowing had been. Today, I know that my first impression of someone is the most valid for me.

Life is a journey, and everything that comes along with it is crucial to our growth. We get what we need. Nothing is ever too little. Nothing is ever too much. God is the Creator of our human family as well as our Spirit family. Both families are here to help us throughout our journey. But we must not forget that God and God alone is everything. God is the Creator. He the Source, the Source of All. He has provided us with all the help that we could ever need. However helpful our spiritual family is to us, we must remember that God is the one deserving of all of the praise and glory. Thank you, God, for our spiritual family. Thank you for designing a perfect plan to assist us through this lifetime and all others to come. Thank you. Thank you. Thank you.

"Relationships are energy, and energy is constantly moving and vibrating."

CHAPTER 9

A COURSE
IN RELATIONSHIPS

THE ONLY ETERNAL relationship whose shape, form, nature and essence has never been altered and never will be altered is the relationship that Our Father in Heaven has with us. All other relationships are temporary. They change course, they change roles, they change purpose, they change shape, they change form. Someone can be with us today in a physical body, and tomorrow they can leave their body and from that moment on are only able to be with us in spirit. Our human family as well as our Spirit family is first and foremost our spiritual family. We may not always like the people in our lives. We may not always enjoy having them around. But it doesn't change the fact that people are part of God's perfect plan for us. Everyone that crosses our path has made a contribution to our lives. They are members of our human and spiritual family. Our human family consists of people who are our master teachers. They can also be our soulmates. And when we have done a lot of inner work, we have the ability to become and attract a twin flame. Upon this Earth, we meet our master teachers, soulmates, and twin flames in the human form. Our human family is just as important as the beings that make up our Spirit family.

Master Teacher

A master teacher is a being with whom we have had the opportunity to work through many important lessons. We usually have had more than one incarnation with them. We recognize these people by the lessons they bring to us and us to them— unconditional love. A master teacher is someone with whom we have a very close relationship, such as a parent or sibling. This relationship usually begins with a family member, although it does not have to. There is a saying that the one we learn the most from is the one that gives us the most trouble. A master teacher is someone who brings us many lessons, usually ones we don't like.

The lessons a master teacher brings to us usually come with lots of pain and heartache. There may be problems with communication, different personality traits, morals, values, and beliefs. You may feel as though you are constantly fighting with this person, wishing he or she could be different. You may find yourself wishing they weren't a part of your life, yet no matter how hard you try, you can't seem to get away from them. The ultimate lesson a master teacher brings is the one of acceptance. In such a relationship, we may feel we have gone through hell and back. But through this relationship, we have the opportunity to learn to love unconditionally and to realize we cannot control other human beings by changing them to fit our image—even if we believe changing them is for the better. When we reach the adult stage, we can have more master teachers, such as a mate, a child, or a spouse's family member. The list increases as life goes on.

Soulmates

Soulmates are people with whom we have incarnated before. They are here with us in this current lifetime because of unfinished business. We are all soulmates to each other, and all of us have more than one soulmate. We start meeting our soulmates in our childhood years. When we meet them, we have an instant feeling of knowing them before. There is no checklist. Only an immediate reaction of like or dislike, comfort or discomfort. Any relationship that brings us strong feelings such as love, dislike, attraction, enjoyment, and connection is a soulmate relationship. We can marry a soulmate and then they become a master teacher for us. In fact, most marriages that occur between soulmates turn the two parties into master teachers for each other. Like the master teachers, soulmates bring us lessons that challenge us to grow and expand our consciousness. But the lessons our soulmates bring to us are less intense than those of the master teacher; therefore, many of our soulmates come and go out of our lives.

Not everyone that crosses our paths is meant to stay with us throughout our entire lifetime. Some people come for a day. Others a week, a month, a year. There are also those that come and never leave. Soulmates do not always come as a love interest. They can show up as friends, parents, teachers, lovers—any role in which we have a close, ongoing relationship. A soulmate is someone to whom we have very familiar energies. We have returned with them in this life together in order to complete unfinished business from past incarnations and to work out certain lessons. Sometimes we come back with love. But we can also come back with feelings of anger and betrayal. In the beginning, like attracts like. There is a feeling of being very comfortable with each other. It can work in the opposite way as well. Each person brings to the relationship what the other one does not.

Relationships are energy, and energy is constantly moving and vibrating. In every relationship, each person has the opportunity to grow and change. Sometimes these changes are compatible with each other. Sometimes they are not. When they are not, each person feels the need to move in a different direction. Usually, the very thing that brought them together is now tearing them apart. This is true in both romantic relationships as well as platonic friendships. People can make the conscious choice of staying in a soulmate relationship even though it is finished. When this occurs, both parties become most miserable. The pain continues to increase until someone reaches the point where they have had enough. The first person to reach this point is usually the one to end the relationship for good. Ending a soulmate relationship can bring feelings of guilt, regret, emptiness, and void. But in time, both parties are able to realize that doing so was for the highest good of all. Both parties are free to move forward and walk the path that works best for them. There is no right way to learn. There is no wrong way to grow. There is only one home: the Father. And all of us have our own way of getting home.

Need-based Relationships

In my work as a life coach and a trans-channel, almost everyone I have met wants to meet "the one." People love talking about finding their other half: the one that is going to fix them, the one that is going to complete them, the one that will make them feel whole. Both men and women have told me how very important it is for them to have a relationship with the one. Therefore, finding the one becomes the major quest of their lives. Their whole being focuses on finding someone to be with. For women, it's usually about being taken care of and being saved. For men, it's usually about being mothered and rescuing someone. For both, it comes down to fulfilling an internal need of being taken care of and feeling safe.

Need-based relationships do not come from love. They come from fear. The fear that one is not enough. At the core of a need-based relationship, there is a belief that one is not equal, that one is not whole, and that one is not complete within themselves. Therefore, one goes on a search outside of themselves to find "the one" that can make them feel equal, whole, and complete. Choosing to participate in a relationship based on need is choosing to enter into an agreement of self-destruction. The desire to fulfill his or her internal need enables the person to give his or her God-given power over to someone else. They give and give until they reach a state of powerlessness. Relationships based on need not only *come* from fear, they are full of it. Completely intertwined in it. Imagine someone who's afraid of being alone. Now, picture the power the other person holds over their partner knowing this about them.

In the years I grew up, I saw my mother become totally dependent upon my father. It didn't matter if she wanted to be with him or not. She had to stay, as she did not want to be alone. She gave all responsibility of herself over to my father.

Then, she complained constantly that she was not happy. My mother went to great lengths to instill in me her belief that all a woman needed to do in her life was catch a man and get married. She could then relax and abdicate all responsibility for herself over to him. Throughout the years, I noticed that even though the women would be supported financially, there would be a high price to pay. I strongly believe I went the opposite way because of what I had learned from my mother. Long ago, I decided I did not want to live my life as she did. I had no desire to depend on anyone else. I saw what it did firsthand to my mother and many other women, and I didn't like it. I have always taken care of myself the best way I knew how. I wasn't always happy. It wasn't always easy. But I have always felt it was my responsibility to take care of myself.

One of the major lessons we are all here to learn is that we are whole and complete and that all of our needs are met with God. Not another person. God has made us whole and complete within ourselves. We don't need anyone. We want someone. That is the difference. It's perfectly fine to want someone in our lives. We weren't created to be all alone. But the idea of needing someone is a lie. God is all we need. We are one with God. In God, we are whole, complete and safe. No one can do that for us but God. We are not to trade our self-worth to other people for the sake of need. God provides us with everything we need at the exact moment we need it. Involvement in need-based relationships follows one theme: I'm not good enough. This is what I deserve. These types of relationships fill no gaps within us. In fact, they create more holes and chaos.

After the initial glow wears off, we are faced with the truth. We see the relationship as it is and not as we want it to be. God wants the best for us always, without exception. And if we are not getting the best there is, it is because we are choosing to give ourselves less than what we deserve. The good news is: we aren't stuck with our choices. We can choose again and again and again. When we feel lonely, empty, and afraid, all we need to do is ask God to come and be with us. God is the best companion there is. He is the only one who truly knows us inside and out. He is the only one who knows exactly what we need.

Abusive Relationships

Some of my clients have been involved in abusive relationships, and I have been baffled at how they convince themselves to remain in the pain. Over the years, I have thought of some of the reasons people have a difficult time leaving abusive relationships, and there have been two major reasons that stand out. The first one is a lack of self-love. Deep down inside, this is the relationship he or she believes they deserve. We accept what we believe we deserve. If we truly believed we deserved better, we would never settle for less. The other reason people stay in abusive relationships is because of the comfort zone. When we are in constant pain, we forget what life is like without having the pain. We get so used to pain and misery that they become second nature. We like the predictability of knowing what to expect. We already know what we have to deal with. Why step into the unknown? Staying in the known, however painful and miserable it is, is less scary than moving out into the unknown. We are afraid to take a risk. We are afraid of getting hurt. We are afraid of getting worse than what we already have. And so, we settle instead of reaching for the stars because we don't believe there are any stars shining out there. And even if there are, we don't believe they are shining for us.

I have asked people in abusive situations the same questions I've had to ask myself. "When is it enough? What has to happen for you to finally be done with this relationship and allow yourself to move on to your greater good?" So many people are unable to answer these questions. It is not for me to tell them the answers. Sometimes the best thing is just to bring these questions to the front of their conscious mind. In time, they will get the answers. Abusive relationships don't need to be physical. Emotional abuse is more damaging to a person than the physical. Bruises heal quickly; emotional wounds do not. I have had many clients, both men and women, who come to me after an abusive relationship that they hated has ended. They sit there, lamenting the end of the relationship. I look straight into their eyes and ask, "What exactly are you missing? Is it the pain? The suffering? What are the tears for?" Most of the time, they stare back at me, unable to say a word.

We stay in abusive relationships because we believe we deserve to suffer. And this is the way we punish ourselves. Both men and women have come to me and were happy as soon as the relationship ended. But after some time passed, usually a day or two, they were miserable. Before they knew it, they were involved in another relationship like the one they had gotten out of or worse. Sometimes, they had no clue how they recycled the relationship. We recreate what we are comfortable with. It's called a comfort zone. As stated before, we are comfortable with it because it is predictable and we know it well. There are no surprises. Therefore, we would rather stay in what we know then move on to what we don't.

Letting go can be a difficult process. It is a process of complete trust and faith. Sometimes the process happens rather quickly and other times it is slow. It depends on how emotionally invested you are in the current situation. If you truly have had enough, you will know. As long as there is a grain of doubt, you have not reached the point of letting go. If this is the case, don't judge yourself. This will only make things worse. Accept yourself where you are. If you are not ready to completely let go, it's all right. Most people are not ready. There is usually one last thing they feel they need to do.

In order to truly end any relationship, everything must be done. All avenues must be exhausted. It is only then that doubt vanishes and is replaced with anticipation.

When people leave an abusive relationship and regret it, I don't believe they miss the person or the relationship. What I feel they are grieving is the end of their dream. For example, some of us get married and believe in the fairy tale of living happily ever after. And we feel like a failure when this doesn't happen. I have found that the struggles we face are never about the other person. They are always about us. We bring to ourselves what we believe we deserve. I have known beautiful, wonderful people who have chosen to go from one abusive relationship to another. We cannot fix other people. We can't even fix ourselves. God fixes us when we allow Him to work in us, through us, as us. There are no loving reasons for us to choose pain and misery for ourselves. We deserve to have everything we desire in our lives. When we believe we are worthy, we will attract someone who will appreciate and love us for who and what we are. We won't have to convince them of this. They will see it on their own. We all are worthy of love. Loving ourselves begins with us.

Twin Flame

I have been asked many times if soulmates and twin flames are the same. They are not. Soulmates and twin flames are very different. They each carry a different vibrational energy. A soulmate is a being who is very familiar to us. They may have taken different roles in other lifetimes, yet their energy vibration is one we recognize. Soulmate marriages can be very happy and successful, although most are not. A twin flame, however, vibrates on a higher energy vibration than a soulmate. Therefore the lessons are on a higher level. There is only one requirement in order to attract a twin flame energy. We must be whole and complete within ourselves. The twin flame relationship is not at all based on need; it is solely based upon desire. Think of two trees intertwined with each other. This is the soul-mate relationship. Now look at two trees that are standing very close together with visible space in between them. This is the twin flame relationship. There is space in between.

Every single being has a twin flame. At the moment of creation, from one came two. I am not talking about a half and a half. I am referring to two complete wholes from one whole. Not all beings desire to have their twin flame come to them in this lifetime. A twin flame is exactly what the name implies. It is the mirror of you. In other words, one cannot be whole and the other a half. A twin flame relationship can only be between two wholes. Each one is there because they choose to be there. They are not asking for the other person to fix them or make them whole. There is a flow to them, and these relationships bring much love and joy to the participants.

A twin flame relationship can only occur when both parties have done much inner work on themselves. It can only occur when a person comes to a place within themselves where they recognize the gift they are. Being a gift is not based upon anything external; it is an inner validation from you to you. Each being has come to the realization of exactly who they are, with certainty. They know their purpose, and are ready to be of service to the Light. They do not need each other for any reason. The relationship is free of fear. Both parties are well aware they are a gift to themselves as well as to the other person. They know clearly what they bring to the relationship, and they are ready and willing to participate. There is an immediate recognition of each other. The gift they give to each other is unconditional love. The twin flame relationship carries no judgment. This means everyone is free to be themselves. No one has a desire to change or fix the other one. This does not mean they have to like all aspects of each other. It means there is no desire to control or manipulate the other person. They accept each other as they are.

Finding the twin flame is finding yourself first. We all have aspects of ourselves that we wish weren't there or that we could change. The twin flame energy is unique to each individual. First, you must see yourself clearly without judgment. If you are judging yourself and feeling less than, you will attract a need-based relationship. Instead of looking at all of the "less" of yourself, begin to look at all of your attributes. Make a list of who you are and what you bring to a relationship. None of us will ever be perfect. But we must acknowledge our change and growth. It's about improvement. Not perfection. I didn't start out believing I was a gift, but I now know and believe in who I am and what I bring to every relationship. This is what's important. Everyone to whom I've explained the twin flame concept to has asked the same question, "Is the person I am involved with my twin flame?" If you have to ask, you already know the answer. When you meet your twin flame, you know it. The twin flame is the mirror of you. It is also possible to have a non-romantic twin flame relationship with someone of the same sex. A love for each other without the physical aspects—a pure soul love. It has taken me many years to make up my mind on whether I desire to meet my male twin flame or not. And I do. I used to have a long list of what my twin flame needed to be. But today, I no longer have a physical type describing what he should look like. I am training myself to look beyond the appearance of the person and instead into their heart. I care deeply about who he is on the inside and the attributes he displays to me. I want him to feel the same way about me as I feel about him. I don't want any more one-sided relationships. I've had enough of those in my life. I have asked God to meet him, and I believe God will bring him in my life. Do I need this to happen in my life? No. Do I desire it? Yes. Very much so!

In the meantime, I am living each day to the best of my ability—one day at a time. I am having fun, and I feel blessed. My life is not perfect. However, it is better than I thought it would ever be. I know God loves me. And I know I'm worthy of God's love. For most of my life I was terrified of meeting myself in someone else. When I first realized the mirror image was about positive as well as negative aspects of myself, it was difficult for me to accept there were attributes I liked about myself. It has taken me many years of going inward and healing the wounds to recognize and accept myself for who I am and not who I think I should be. To me this is the definition of the mirror image and the importance it plays in my life. I am no longer afraid of being vulnerable with someone. I am learning to trust myself more and more and to trust God as well. I know God loves me and wants the best for me. All I need to do is simply be. I can be authentic—the real me. The greatest gift is that I know myself and I really like myself. In fact, I would love to have a male version of me in my life.

Sometimes the twin flame doesn't meet our physical image of what we want. This gives us the opportunity to grow beyond our limitations, or stay where we are. We always retain the choice. We can bring in our twin flame and still we do not have to enter into a relationship with them. Both people have an equal right to make the decision to enter into a relationship or not. If one or both say no, another twin flame will be brought in. Remember, the twin flame is about you bringing in you. Sometimes we think we are ready, only to realize we are not. In the world of Spirit there is always abundance, and that means more. We cannot and will not miss out on what is ours. There is always more. What is ours cannot be taken by anyone else.

Whatever we decide for ourselves, whether it be the soulmate or twin flame, it makes no difference. We just have to enjoy it and stop needing it. We don't have to settle. We can have it all. In the world of God, there is enough for everyone. We can all have our heart's desires. All we need to do is allow it to happen. Relax, and let life reveal on life's terms, not ours. We have to learn to put aside our choices and ask for God's choice for us. Asking for God's choice is to trust and know God. To know God is to know ourselves. We are never going to be perfect or do everything perfectly. It will not happen. We can, however, love ourselves no matter what. Everyone comes with stuff. I do and so do you. The question is, will my stuff be compatible with your stuff? Am I better off without you than with you? Is your presence in my life contributing to my greatest good? We don't have to figure out all the answers all at once. Everything will reveal in time, when we are patient and ready to see the truth. The truth always comes out.

"Earth is governed by processes that are spiritually based."

CHAPTER 10

THE JOURNEY OF LIFE

I REMEMBER GROWING up wanting so badly to be a teenager. By the time I was a teen, I wanted to be an adult. It has taken me many years to realize that life is not about the next place where I end up, or about reaching the next stage. It's about the journey that takes me there. The journey of life is filled with many surprises. Sometimes these surprises are as sweet as honey. Other times, life leaves us with a sour taste no amount of honey can get rid of. The good, the bad, the ugly, are all equally important. Without the rain, who would know how to enjoy the sunlight? Without the sunlight, who would know how to enjoy the fresh air that comes after the rain?

Throughout my own life journey, I've come to learn that no matter how hard I try, I will never fully understand the mind of God. God is beyond human understanding. How does one explain the

Earth rotating on itself every twenty-four hours? How does one comprehend the Earth revolving around the sun every three hundred and sixty-five days? God is the Ultimate Creator, the Ultimate Engineer. Everything in His realm is done perfectly. And it is all done in Divine Order.

Divine Order is another concept that is beyond human explanation. Tomas has explained to me that Divine Order resides in the realm of Spirit and is not affected by the laws of man. Timing is everything and God's timing is not based upon linear time such as we know it here on Earth. Linear time means sixty seconds in a minute, sixty minutes in an hour, twenty-four hours in a day, seven days in a week, four weeks in a month, and twelve months in a year. God's time is based on one thing only: Divine Order. It means when the being is ready, the opportunity will present itself at the exact moment the being needs it. It will not appear one second early. Or one second late.

The Higher Self

The Higher Self is the part of us that knows better. It is our direct link to Spirit. The Higher Self has one purpose and that is to govern Divine Order. The Higher Self selects the lessons at the exact moment we are ready for them. We choose our lessons. But we do not control when they come. Picture this. Over our shoulders is a fine net with many holes. In each hole, there is a rolled paper.

There are thousands of these papers around us and each one of them is a lesson. When the Higher Self selects a lesson, it comes out of the hole and enters through the top of the head, called the crown. The lesson then travels downward until it comes to the solar plexus, the area under the breast, sometimes called the seat of emotions. The lesson then manifests itself into our physical reality. This is the reason Tomas always says, "The outside is created from the inside, first."

Life is about experiences. Experiences are about the lessons we need to learn. We are brought everything we need to experience the lesson, such as the person and the circumstance. We then have the choice to take on the lesson or not. If we decline the lesson, it will just reappear at another time. Though we don't control when they come, we maintain control as to whether or not we choose to learn the lessons.

The Process of Creation

The life we currently have, however we feel about it, is the life we have created for ourselves. We have created this life by focusing. Focus is a very powerful tool of creation. It is the spiritual law that directly connects us to our power. We can control our reality because our reality is the universe within us that is then manifested out. The universe within us is made up of what we think and believe. Therefore, if we don't like our reality, all we need to do is change our inner thoughts and belief system. When we do so, our outer reality will automatically reshape from our inner world.

Thoughts create. Whatever it is that you continuously think about, whether you want it or not, you will create it. The universe creates directly from what you are thinking and doing. The more you think of something, the faster you will create it for yourself. Focus is like a laser beam of light. If you look at a laser, you will see it is a small yet intense beam of light. What makes it so powerful is its intensity. The broader the beam of light, the weaker it becomes. Focus is the laser of our mind. The universe does not think—it creates. When you worry, you are focusing on what you do not want. In creating, the universe doesn't say, "He or she doesn't really want this." It says, "Look at all of the energy he or she is giving this. We will create this for him or her." Then, wham! Just like that, we have the very thing we didn't want right at the center of our lives. So many of us are confused when it comes to creating. We have it backwards. We think our reality is created from outside of us. Not true. It is totally an inside job. Whatever we give to ourselves, we will give out to everyone else.

Earth is governed by processes that are spiritually based. These spiritual laws are carved in stone and never change. Once you understand the processes that govern life, you have the key to open the door to understanding the universe we live in and how it works. These laws govern our reality—both the inner and outer worlds. Change always comes from the inside. I have learned nothing on the outside needs to change except my thoughts about it. Sometimes the change is quick and other times it is not. Time does not matter; the outside will eventually change to match the inside. Sometimes the changes we make in our lives affect the people around us and they might be uncomfortable with these shifts. If they choose to go, let them. Others will come in to mirror and support these changes. Willingness is key to change. Without willingness, nothing will change. We will just stay stuck in the same habits. Repetition is instrumental in establishing a new habit. Action is most important too. Keep doing it and don't worry about the results.

Visualization is an incredible tool. I have used it and it works. See whatever it is you desire happening with you in the picture and eventually it will manifest. Desire is one thing and doing it is something else. Doing is the key to manifestation. The result always stays with God. Upon this Earth, we are very familiar with the term "law." We have many laws, and they are always shifting and changing. The term "universal law" is the exact opposite. A universal law is written in stone and will never change. Throughout eternity, it remains as it is written. Some of these laws are: "Physical reality is created from the inside out," and "Thoughts create through focus," and "There is a Divine Order in life," and "We will never understand the mind of God in human form," and "Life will become easy when we get into the flow."

These laws have never and will never change. When we go against the flow, life becomes difficult. We become weary and no matter what we do, life does not work in our favor. Processes are part of the flow. When we get in tune with them, life becomes easy and effortless instead of hard and challenging. There is a law for creating. Some people call it "manifestation." Everything in life is a process. There is also a process for creating and a process for healing. Understanding the processes will allow you to establish new patterns that will bring you peace. Like baking a cake, all of the ingredients must be present for the cake to form correctly. If the cake is put into the oven and something is missing, it will not turn out the way it was intended to. It is important to have all of the ingredients needed for the success of the cake. The universe works in a similar way. Time, energy, and focus are needed in the creation process. Processes are put into place by the universe and they do not change. They always work in the same way and in the same order. To understand some of these processes is to accelerate our healing in order to change our lives.

The Three A's of Change

Awareness is the first step toward change. You cannot change something you are not aware of. Awareness is having a clear picture of our reality the way it is and not the way we want it to be. Awareness is a great motivator. Have you ever met someone who was in so much pain you could see it on their face? Yet, they didn't seem to know this or want to do anything to change it. Most people are unaware of what to do to change. I have a friend who calls these people "the walking dead." Without awareness, we become captive of our feelings and behavior. We create a prison of our own making. Thankfully, this isn't permanent. The wonderful news is that we have the key that opens the door to our freedom anytime we choose to use it. The key is to become aware and be willing to change.

The second step in changing is **acceptance**. Tomas describes acceptance as the definition of love. Acceptance does not mean we have to like or dislike our situation. It only means we have to acknowledge our situation and love ourselves through it. When I am able to accept, I am a much happier person. Acceptance keeps me moving forward in my life. The ego, the small child mind, is not our friend. It constantly asks "Why?" Have you ever been with a small child and all that they ever said as an answer was, "Why?" and at the end of the conversation, you were angry or frustrated? Our conscious mind is like that. There is never enough proof or information to satisfy it. It is an ongoing "why," without an end. Acceptance is ownership of one's actions, without asking "why?" Spirit will never address a question when asked with "Why?" It will only address questions that are expressed with "What?" and "How?" Asking why keeps us stuck. Asking what and how keeps us moving forward. "What" is a word of action and "how" moves us into action, which is the third step in change.

Even if we become aware and we accept, nothing will change without **action**. The question now becomes, "What do I do, and how do I do it?" We can use words all we want, but without the action to accompany them, nothing will change. Any new action is better than none at all. The universe will always support action when coming from the heart. If we continue to do what we've always done, nothing will change. I have sometimes found myself thinking that I don't know what else to do, so I will keep doing what I am familiar with. I remember when I gave up smoking. I did not know what to do with my hands. I was so used to smoking and holding the cigarette that I almost went back to smoking because of it. I finally had to find something else to do with my hands. I put them in my pockets. I had to make sure the clothes I wore had pockets. It worked! Now, years later, I no longer worry about what to do with my hands, and I have never gone back to smoking.

Every choice we make is based on an intention. Intention always precedes action. Intention is also based on self-esteem. When our self-esteem is high, we make loving choices for ourselves. When it is low, we make choices that lead us to pain and suffering. It does not matter if we are aware of our true intention or not. The results of our actions will show us what our intention was when we made our choice. Results are directly connected to intention and self-esteem. If we like what we are getting, we will continue to do the same action, regardless of the results. Our words may be different, but the saying "actions speak louder than words" is true. Our core beliefs drive every action we do. The results of these actions tell us what our core beliefs are. There are only two core beliefs, and both are based solely upon our self-esteem. When we feel good with the results of our actions, we have a higher level of self-esteem. If we don't like our results, our beliefs are coming from low self-esteem.

A Never-Ending Journey

Life is a never-ending journey of experiences: learning, sharing, growing, and changing. As long as we are in the body, there will never be a time when we graduate through this thing called life and are able to sit back and relax. Throughout my own life's journey, I have cried enough tears to run me a river. I have also laughed so loud that all of my laughter could combine into one of the loudest echoes on Earth. I made many mistakes along the way, for which I am most glad. How else would have I learned? I truly believe I have learned most from the things I believed I did wrong rather than the things I thought I did right. But through all of my trials and tribulations, I've learned that life has a way of working itself out. I look back sometimes at my darkest moments and laugh wholeheartedly. I laugh because these moments are behind me. I laugh because they have taught me so much. I laugh because without them I would not be where I am today.

AFTERWORD

My heart is full of gratitude for the blessings and gifts God has bestowed upon me. I am living a life that is beyond my wildest imagination. I have met wonderful people and experienced countless events that are nothing short of miracles. Finishing this book is a miracle in itself. It has been worked on for over fifteen years, and now it is finally time to share it with the world. I don't know where this book will go or who will read it or how they will feel about it. What I do know is that God is in charge of my life and everything that manifest in it. I do my part. The results rest with God. My prayer for myself as well as for everyone else is to stay peaceful and close to God. It is only with God that we are truly safe. May we rest in God's love and mercy. May we remember on our brightest day as well as our darkest hour that God loves us unconditionally.

ACKNOWLEDGEMENTS

My deepest thanks to all of those who have expended time and energy in creating this work of truth. My special thanks to C P Beauvoir, who has chosen to become the vehicle for this holy endeavor. Thank you for choosing to open yourself to the truths that are written in this literature.

ABOUT THE AUTHORS

Helenne Deutscher

Originally from New York, Helenne has been living in Florida since 1956. Helenne has worked for large global corporations and has owned her own businesses. In conjunction with maintaining her private practice, she is a consultant, providing leadership training and business coaching to individuals and teams. Helenne's client base extends to individuals, children, and families. Helenne also develops and conducts leadership classes and life seminars.

The Reluctant Channel is about her spiritual journey and the amazing events that have transformed her life. The information given to Helenne allows her to help others learn the spiritual laws that govern life. Understanding how the universe works assists us in a clear and simple way with transforming ourselves, which in turn transforms our lives. This method, based on spiritual truths and the inner self, is most effective. Helenne has been the channel for this information and has been sharing her knowledge with others for the last twenty-five years.

www.HelenneDeutscher.com

C P Beauvoir

C P Beauvoir was born in Port-au-Prince, Haiti. She moved to the United States when she was thirteen years old. She has been writing all her life. She is currently working on a series of books, which is coming to completion. C P Beauvoir is delighted to have co-authored this book as she wholeheartedly believes in it.

www.cpbeauvoir.com